TO INFORM
OR TO CONTROL?

TO INFORM
OR TO CONTROL?

The New Communications Networks

OSWALD H. GANLEY
GLADYS D. GANLEY

McGraw-Hill Book Company
New York   St. Louis   San Francisco   Toronto   Hamburg   Mexico

1 2 3 4 5 6 7 8 9 D O D O 8 7 6 5 4 3 2

ISBN 0-07-022761-6

LIBRARY OF CONGRESS CATALOGING IN PUBLICATION DATA

Ganley, Oswald Harold, 1929–
To inform or to control?
1. Telecommunication.   2. Telecommunication
policy.   I. Ganley, Gladys D.   II. Title.
HE7631.G23   384'.068   81–20748
ISBN 0–07–022761–6   AACR2

Book design by Nancy Dale Muldoon.

TO OUR CHILDREN,
Robert and Delia

Preface

AT first glance the topics dealt with in this book may appear to be a string of different subjects with only minor or perhaps no relationships to each other. The assembly of a whole picture from these apparently disparate fragments is the purpose of this book.

Over the past few decades, the responsibilities and interests of all our leaders—in government, in businesses, in industries, and in universities—have become increasingly specialized and categorized. Hence, when a tidal wave like that produced by computers, communications, and information sweeps through, each leader sees only some minute part of it. Even as the foundations of his most vital interests are being torn away by the flood, he remains unaware that his castle is crumbling. Or even as opportunities pile up before him, he ignores them in the struggle to shore up traditional infrastructures.

What we are witnessing on every hand today is the beginning of the collapse of economies based on traditional industries, *traditionally managed,* and the rise of economies based on or assisted by new communications and information resources. These economies are first of all global and only sec-

ondarily national. For communications and information resources have moved great blocks of activity beyond national
borders. Whole industries, businesses, money markets, currency flows, banking, energy resources, and defense systems—
and communications and information itself—have gone global.
Most of our stakes are now global. But governments have
not gone global. Many groups now operate outside the framework of nation states, and certain events have escaped national
control. Still, we can expect that for the foreseeable future
the *responsibility*, if not the *power*, to decide and to arbitrate
will continue to rest with the nation state.

The story of communications and information has recently
changed radically, so we have begun at the beginning. We
think it is important for our readers to know the physical
armamentarium of what amounts to a revolution and how it
is presently deployed. We want them to be able to see the
ferment which is building in the United States domestically,
and the often different ferment taking place abroad. We want
them to sense the collision course.

We show the reader how areas of domestic U.S. activity
which once had boundaries are now flowing like lava into
each other. We describe the domestic roadblocks they meet,
which used to be helpful channels, and which were devised
long ago to serve other purposes.

We jump across the U.S. border and take up several specific
international problem areas. All of these are of a nature vital
to the very survival of the United States in a position of global
leadership. And all are merely symptomatic of what is to come.

We then relate these activities to the broad geopolitical
areas of interest to the United States: the industrialized countries, the developing countries, and the communist countries.
We give one case history, that of the relationships of the United
States and Canada, as they range across the broad communications and information spectrum. We find, in this single instance, that new communications and information developments are prominent in whatever we do and actively affect
events both positively and negatively.

And we have found this to be true wherever we have looked, on both a domestic and a global basis: in industry, in manufacturing, in banking, in currency markets, in business, in government, in transportation, in recreation, in trade, in defense, in security, in arms control, in intelligence gathering, in terroristic activities—you name it.

There is no end to the opportunities now opening up, and no simple answers to arising problems. All the king's horses and all the king's men cannot supply the answers today, for most of the questions have yet to be formulated. This book describes the situation as we enter the 1980s, which will be a decade of worldwide change. It points to the broad routes these changes will take, and erects certain signposts along the way.

Acknowledgments

THE authors gratefully acknowledge the assistance of Professor Anthony G. Oettinger, and thank him for his unceasing encouragement and guidance as this book developed. We have leaned heavily on the basic concepts of the Program on Information Resources Policy and its publications over an extended time span.

Special thanks go also to William Read, Herman Pollack, and Morris Crawford for their intricate readings of the draft manuscripts as they progressed and for sharing their own unique experience and insights with us.

We also thank the following persons, who have reviewed drafts or have otherwise shared their ideas and information with us: James Armstrong, Richard Barnes, Mari Ann Blatch, Justin Bloom, Harvey Brooks, Robert Chartrand, William Colby, Edward David, Hugh Donaghue, Stephen Doyle, Geza Feketekute, Brant Free, Arthur Freeman, Harry Freeman, Wreatham Gathright, Susan Gordon, Jonathan Gunther, James Harding, Norman Hinerfeld, Donald Hollis, Fred Irving, Wayne Kay, George Kroloff, Eric Novotny, William Odom, Per Ongstadt, Joseph Pelton, Larry Povich, Peter Robinson,

Hewsam Ryan, William Salmon, Naomi Seligman, Wells Stabler, Ronald Stowe, Raymond Vernon, and Eugene Yeates.

These persons are not, however, responsible for or necessarily in agreement with the views expressed herein, nor should they be blamed for any errors of fact or interpretation.

OSWALD H. GANLEY
GLADYS D. GANLEY

Contents

Illustrations

". . . Communication can be an instrument of power, a revolutionary weapon, a commercial product, or a means of education; it can serve the ends of either liberation or of oppression, of either the growth of the individual personality or of drilling human beings into uniformity. Each society must choose the best way to approach the task facing all of us and to find the means to overcome the material, social and political constraints that impede progress."

From the Final Report of the MacBride Commission,
UNESCO, Belgrade, Fall 1980

"We can either work to shape, in a wise and effective manner, the changes that now engulf the world or, by acting unwisely, become shackled by them."

Cyrus R. Vance, Former Secretary of State,
Harvard Commencement Address, June 5, 1980

THE BIRTH OF A NEW ECONOMIC SECTOR

Part I

The Challenge to America*

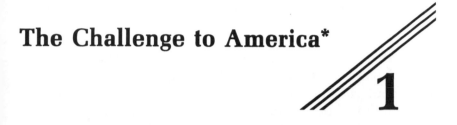

THROUGHOUT the 1960s, and especially the 1970s, vast changes have been taking place within the U.S. electronics industry which have directly affected communications and information. In a climate of general economic gloom, innovation after innovation has leaped forth: in computers, microprocessors, semiconductors, and chip technology; in telecommunications, digitization, packet switching, microwave, laser, and fiber optics; and in the electronic media, cable television and television-related devices. In space electronics, a whole new realm of communications and information devices has linked the globe, with the advent of satellites for navigation, weather, communications, remote sensing, and military and security uses.

These electronic innovations have moved the communications and information industries rapidly forward, even as many more traditional industries have stagnated and declined. And they have spilled over and met with similar burgeoning, though not yet quite so advanced, electronics industries in

* With apologies to Jean Jacques Servan-Schreiber's *The American Challenge* of the late 1960s.[1]

the rest of the industrialized world. Overnight, the developing nations have embraced the electronic advance parties—transistor radios, recording cassettes, and television—and are joining the INTELSAT satellite communications system in droves. Meanwhile, U.S. communications and information resources have been met head on by the technological brain children of the Soviet Union.

And yet, the opportunities and the upheaval which must inevitably occur with such vast changes, both within the United States domestically and in its international relations, have gone virtually unnoticed by U.S. leaders. The press, business, industry, the Congress, and government policy makers began to recognize only a scant two or three years ago that anything at all was afoot. And when they noticed, they tended to focus on a single tree in the varied communications and information forest.

The economic importance of communications and information resources for the 1980s and after cannot be overrated. While the cost of other goods and services is rising astronomically, the cost of communications and information is radically falling. In the five-year period 1974–1979, computer costs fell 95 percent. Markets are proliferating in telecommunications, data processing, office management equipment and services, broadcasting, satellite activities, electronic fuel-saving systems, and even in electronic toys. One source projects a U.S. domestic communications and information market of $100 billion by 1985, and another gives a world market figure of at least $325 billion by 1988. There are speculations to even $500 billion by the end of the decade. Other astonishing figures abound.[2]

More important even than the computer to these markets are microprocessors: tiny chips with many of the computer's powers. Benjamin Rosen, an electronics analyst for Morgan Stanley & Company, is said by the *New York Times* to believe that:[3] ". . . the world market for integrated circuits will grow from $5 billion this year (1979) to $80 billion by the turn of the century."

While the communications and information industries are

The projected launch of one of a series of INTELSAT V's by the space shuttle.
(National Aeronautics and Space Administration [NASA.])

forming an important economic sector in themselves, they are simultaneously serving as tools to revolutionize traditional industries. The activities of the print media, of banks and other financial institutions, of world currency markets, of postal systems, and of the steel, petroleum, construction, transportation, and consumer goods industries are being rapidly transformed. Those businesses not adjusting are being left behind or being usurped by newcomers more adept at turning electronic innovations to their advantage.

A wholly new set of dynamics has thus been put in motion, within both the domestic U.S. economy and the economies in other parts of the world. Many of the European countries and Japan are already staging formidable communications and information revolutions of their own. The sudden success of the Japanese automobile market in the United States was due in no small part to Japan's imaginative and skillful use of computers and microprocessors to control everything from steel production to auto parts production and assembly, and to the functions of the automobile itself.

With these new electronic communications and information tools, the United States now communicates in real time around the globe, enjoys instant reporting of news of far-off events, spreads its media products to every corner of the earth, discovers the world's hidden resources, keeps watch on its adversaries to protect itself and its allies, and aids in arms control and peacekeeping.

Almost no facet of life globally remains untouched by these new resources. But such profound changes cannot take place without profound disturbances. Regulatory balances and established competitive trade situations are upset. Methods of making financial arrangements are changed. Legal principles and concepts of sovereign rights and national borders are challenged. Social upheavals and shifts in employment patterns are created. Cultural resentments are fomented. The ways in which war and peace are waged are altered. The functions of domestic and worldwide institutions are put in question. And, in the military sphere, a communications and information race has developed between the two superpowers.

The price of great new opportunities is already being demonstrated by a growing set of problems concerning privacy and freedom of information, transborder data flow, free flow of news, orbital space for satellites, radio-frequency allocations, the lack of communications opportunities for the developing nations, the use of communications for terroristic activities, blackmail, and governmental overthrow, electronic spying on civilians, vital technology transfer to other countries, and the ownership of outer space.

The $50-trillion-a-year world currency market has been radically altered and now operates 24 hours a day. Former Secretary of the Treasury Michael Blumenthal has said:[4] "We did not appreciate early and fully enough the potential for trouble in the currency market. . . . We did not understand the impact of electronic communications. . . ."

The realization that foreign currency markets never close down anymore—that when those in New York shut, those in Asia and Europe open—brings with it the next realization: that national monies may have, in many ways, escaped national control.

Revolutionary tactics have also changed. The Iranian revolution in 1979 demonstrated innovative ways to use easily available new electronic means like dry copiers, tape recorders, long-distance dialing, and satellite broadcasts to take over and maintain the control of states. In the Iranian hostage crisis of 1979–1980, in a sense diplomatic events were hostage to the international news media and diplomacy was conducted by reporters.

In the face of such obvious opportunities and risks, it would seem logical for the United States both to organize itself domestically and to take an international lead. But American preparation for such a undertaking is sorely flawed. Neither the U.S. government nor the private sector operates in a sufficiently comprehensive fashion to deal with a phenomenon which is fundamentally changing the way they are accustomed to conducting their affairs.

The Canadians have given a lot of thought to such fundamental changes, and Deputy Minister of the Canadian Department of Communications Pierre Juneau puts it thus:[5] "This change . . . reaches to the very heart of the structures of our society: . . . . To the way business is organized, the way government is conducted, money changes hands, products are made, leisure is enjoyed, and . . . how people are informed."

With the exception of atomic energy, the United States concept of the role of any sort of technology in international relations is only about two decades old. That this role is still very poorly understood by U.S. leaders, and has never been integrated into the political, economic, cultural, and social sectors of policymaking and application demonstrates the hurdles communications and information concepts must jump.

No small part of the problem has been American overconfidence. United States technological and general economic superiority has been taken for granted since World War II. That superiority—won partly by default—was maintained for many years primarily because the United States had virtually no challengers.

But it is impossible not to see the challengers now. Military, security, and energy needs are putting vast strains on U.S. power. The value of the dollar is down. United States military strength is no longer unquestioned; U.S. political concepts are not so popular as they once were; nor is U.S. opinion so highly respected. There has been a serious psychological breakdown domestically in the former highly successful cooperation between U.S. universities, businesses, and agencies of government. In most U.S. industries, innovation has slowed. Indeed, the innovative spirit which was America's hallmark has in a way been captured and improved on elsewhere, most notably in Japan.

And basic philosophical challenges are coming to the fore. André Giraud, the French Minister of Industry, made this comment:[6]

I feel that I should stress a problem which the various countries will have to face as the new methods of access to information become widespread. These are the changes which will ensue for the news media and the precautions which will have to be taken to protect the pluralistic and democratic values they uphold. The various parties dealing with information will have to redefine their role in the light of technological change, if democracy is to be preserved.

Communications and information is a fresh, new area where opportunities are wide open. The uses of these resources in the service of development, to stimulate and produce trade, for education, for peacekeeping, for world cooperation—indeed, for the formation of a truly global society—are virtually limitless.

The United States now has the option to interest itself in communications and information resources across the board. If it chooses, it can provide the leadership so necessary for the orderly progression of the information age. If it declines this leadership, the world will not wait. The option will merely pass to other, possibly less benign global forces.

From Scarcity to Abundance

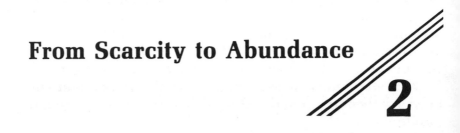

2

INFORMATION has always traveled by the fastest or most convenient means for communicating it, whether that be by speaking, yelling, smoke signaling, beating drums, sending a runner with a message, entrusting a note to a packet boat, the pony express, or a carrier pigeon; posting or flashing lights; writing, printing, and distributing books, newspapers, and magazines; or making use of the postal system.

Whether the information was spoken, handwritten, printed with ink, or recorded on wax, film, or magnetic tape, the purpose has always been the same: To take whatever information was available and convey it to someone for social, informative, entertainment, educational, financial, commercial, political, or military ends. In this sense, nothing has ever changed.

New Technologies Spew Forth

Communications and information resources cover a broad spectrum and are of varying ages. Printing with movable type and books, more or less as we know them, have been available for half a millennium. Newspapers have been around for more than 300 years. Benjamin Franklin put the white space around advertising to make it more attractive in the eighteenth century. The telegraph is 135 years old. The telephone has had its centennial. The camera, then movies, came into being in the nineteenth century, as did various recording devices. The first photograph was reproduced in a newspaper by the halftone process in 1880. Commercial radio arrived in the 1920s and radar prior to World War II. We have had transatlantic communication by telegraph since 1865, by radio since 1927, and by telephone cable since 1956. Microwave relay was developed in World War II and brought into U.S. national telecommunications use shortly thereafter. Television and the first computers made their debut in the 1940s. Then, from the invention of the transistor, which became available in the 1950s, there has been a spewing forth of a multiplicity of devices for handling communications and information by ever more efficient electronic means.

Communications and information resources have from the first coexisted, complemented, cooperated, and competed with each other. With the arrival of each new resource, there has been a spate of speculations that nothing will ever be the same again. And to a large extent, this has been true. Once available, new methods of communications have been rapidly adopted, and earlier, clumsier, and more expensive means have been relegated to lesser or different roles. Few die altogether, but their niche in human affairs suffers change, unless they themselves upgrade and modernize.

Dire predictions have usually been made that this is the end of life as it has been known and that threats are being posed to the power of one group or another. And this, too, has been true. The uneducated have been educated and have secured their liberty from religious or political oppressors in consequence. That which was accessible only to a chosen few has been made accessible to the many. This is a fact not congenial to elite groups. There is no doubt that availability of information through communications—like the availability of any other mass product—is a potent democratizing force. This is the reason why dictatorships limit the availability of newspapers and why the USSR forbids the use of photocopying machines.

Fears for jobs have been omnipresent whenever changes in technology take place, and they have been justified. Those employed in one sort of communications concern have often found themselves jobless. Conversely, new types of jobs have sprung up in the new concerns, which offered more opportunity in the long run. What did the first telephone operators do for a living before the advent of the telephone? They were telegraph boys—subsequently put out of work! And what will telephone operators do for a living as the computer takes over? They will move on to the next rung of the next ladder.

A study of 31 U.S. industries recently showed the top three in total productivity to be the telecommunications industry, the electricity and electronics equipment industry, and the semiconductor industry group. Full-time jobs are reported to have almost doubled in the telecommunications and electricity and electronics equipment industries between the end of the 1940s and 1976. There was an almost 31-fold increase in employment in the semiconductor industry between 1954 and 1974. This study also showed that, contrary to popular opinion, when the rate of change in technology and productivity was rising, unemployment was falling, and vice versa. *Business Week* has estimated that three of the four top high-tech growth areas for the period 1980 to 1990 will be robots, personal computers, and semiconductors. And Fall 1981 Department of Labor statistics indicate that jobs in these areas will grow accordingly. Five of the six areas where jobs will grow fastest in the next decade will be related to computers, they say. As many as 172,000 data-processing-machine mechanics will be needed in 1990, where 63,500 were needed in 1978—an increase of 148 percent. By the late 1980s, the need for computer-systems analysts will grow about 108 percent, computer operators 88 percent, computer programmers 74 percent, and other related jobs about 81 percent.[1]

The new thing being witnessed in communications and information resources right now is a matter of speed, interaction,

GROWTH OF SEMICONDUCTOR TECHNOLOGY

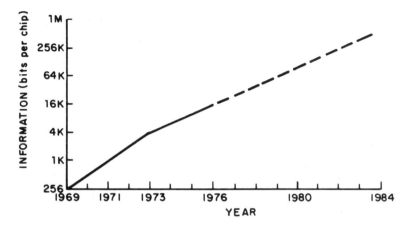

The capacity of the individual microchip has just about doubled each year since 1960. It is in microprocessors—chips with many of the powers of the computer—that the real economic future of communications and information lies. (From *Science and Technology: A Five-Year Outlook*, W. H. Freeman and Company. Copyright © 1979 by the National Academy of Sciences. Reprinted by permission.)

and scope. The United States, followed by the rest of the industrialized world, is moving from an era of relative scarcity in these resources to an era of extreme abundance. The last two decades have seen the rapid development of new communications and information technologies largely based on electronics:

- Photographic duplication processes permit the instant reproduction of printed matter.
- Facsimile allows easy transmission to distant points.
- Cassettes record and play back voices and music, and thanks to transistors, can be taken to and used anywhere in the world.
- News is sent electronically from worldwide sources, and newspapers are printed by photographic means far from the site where news is gathered or analyzed, or the papers mocked up.

- Satellites pick up and deliver all types of information in real time. They also sense and photograph the earth from space.
- Television programs are produced and disseminated by a wide variety of means. Direct broadcasting by satellite lies in the immediate future.
- Fiber optics carry messages converted to light signals around corners and over long distances with great efficiency.
- Microprocessors, which ten years ago could get only 16 bits (pieces of information) on a silicon chip, have a predicted capacity of 256,000 bits by 1984.
- Smaller and smaller and cheaper and cheaper computers which do more and more are rapidly becoming available. Portable minicomputers may be as common within the next decade as handheld calculators are right now.
- Electronics guide missiles, and our defense systems are permeated with telemeters,* warning devices, observation satellites, and electronic listening posts.

The Computer as Workhorse

Leading the communications and information resources parade, since it is essential to many if not most of the new electronics activities, is the computer. Harvard Professor Anthony Oettinger explains the ingenious mathematical concepts which, combined with electronics, have made the digital computer the workhorse of the information world:[2]

The traditional method of dealing with numbers is in an analog way. The number 3.28 is shown as a spot on a ruler, using the distance from the ruler's left edge as the analog of that quantity. The fundamental thing about the analog world is that it is limited by the accuracy with which physical measurements can be made. There is no way to make a physical measurement precise enough to go more than 8 or 9 decimal places. The strength of the digital method is that numbers can be written to any degree of accuracy simply by adding another place. There is an infinity of places off

---

* Telemeters measure distances to and certain characteristics of objects, such as pressure, speed, and temperature. They then transmit the information gathered by radio to distant stations, where it is recorded.

to the left for writing larger and larger numbers, and places off to the right for writing numbers which are increasingly finely chopped. The binary business is simply a modern technological accident that says it's an awful lot easier to build digital devices with an alphabet of two than with an alphabet of any other number. More than two would be nice, but is difficult to maintain in a stable, economical way. It is much easier to decide whether to make a hole or no hole than it is to punch very delicately a half a hole's worth. A hole or no hole is stable as all get out.

The new communications and information technologies are not only swift and efficient, but they are also miraculously

CHANGING COSTS OVER THE NEXT DECADE

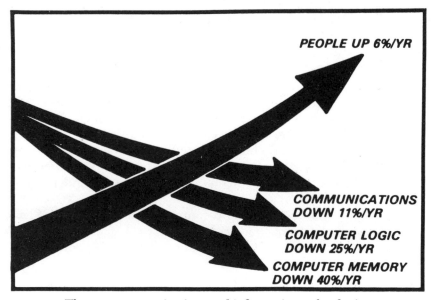

The new communications and information technologies are not only swift and efficient, they are also miraculously cheap. While the cost of just about everything else is rising, these costs are going down. (From Edward W. Scott, "Multifunction Application at a Medium/ Large Site," *Automated Business Communications,* International Data Corporation, Waltham, Mass., April 1979. Reprinted by permission.)

cheap. By 1990, for instance, the computer's upper logic speed will have increased 10,000 times over that of 1979, while its logic costs will have been cut 40 times and its memory costs 400. This annual 40 percent compound savings has been in effect all along. Applied equivalently to the automobile, the sort of Cadillac which cost $10,000 in 1947 could already be bought today for $5. By 1990 it could be had for 50 cents. And if that 1990 Cadillac incorporated the same performance improvements as the computer, it would get 3000 miles to a gallon of gasoline and run about the world at an average speed of 10,000 miles per hour.[3]

There are also similar examples based on the Rolls Royce auto and the Concorde airplane which use the same logic and make the same point.

The following are some computer statistics.[4]

- In 1953 there were 50 existing computers. In 1975, there were 155,000, in 1980, 300,000, and by 1985 there will be 500,000. With the production of smaller, more varied, and more versatile computers, there is no end in sight. This is a business where IBM, in the 1950s, estimated its best potential at 50 new customers!
- In 1953, the computer—with a capacity of a little hand-held calculator today—cost $3 million, weighed a ton, filled a large room, and used the energy of an electric locomotive. The price of a sleek 370/125 is now $500,000, and of a desk model, under $10,000.
- In 1952, one hundred thousand computer calculations cost $1.25. In 1980, one hundred thousand computer calculations cost .0025 cents, or four hundred thousand calculations for a penny.
- Memory capacity per dollar of rental value grew 43.5 times from 1952 to 1970, 80 times by 1977, and will have grown 800 times by 1985.

In the period between December 1974 and December 1979, the cost of hamburger rose 74 percent, of gasoline, more than 100 percent, of building materials, 65 percent. Meanwhile, computing costs *fell* 95 percent. While the price of sending a letter increased from $2.44 in 1965 to $5.50 in

1979,* and "people" costs in general rose by at least 6 percent a year to that time, computing/communications costs dropped by 11 percent a year, computer logic costs by 25 percent a year, and computer memory costs by 40 percent a year. The computer industry itself employs more than three-quarters of a million people in the United States and creates employment for many more.[5]

Communications and the Chip

Within the United States it is expected that data communications equipment markets will experience tremendous future growth. Installed data communications equipment in the United States at the end of 1978 was valued at more than $3 billion. This is expected to increase 2.5 times—to $8 billion—by the end of 1983. This is a compound growth rate of approximately 21 percent a year. Data communications revenues grew from $1.5 billion in the mid-1960s to $4 billion in 1973, to $5.5 billion in 1975, and are expected to reach $22 billion by 1985. Small wonder that pitched battles over computers and their software and data processing services markets are being fought around the world.[6]

FRED BASSET   **by Alex Graham**

Even Fred appreciates the chip. (FRED BASSET by Alex Graham, Dist. Field Newspaper Syndicate, 1980. Copyright © Associated Newspapers Group Ltd. Reprinted by permission.)

* This includes preparation time, typing, paper, and postage.

Silicon—the most abundant element next to oxygen in the earth's crust—forms a layer of quartz on its surface when heated with oxygen present. This quartz, which acts midway between a conductor and an insulator—as a semiconductor—can be etched in controlled patterns. The resulting "chips" not only are vastly smaller than "old-fashioned" transistors (which won their inventors a Nobel prize for being so revolutionary in the 1950s)[7] but are much less prone to being degraded. Beginning with one transistor per chip in 1960, the number of transistors per chip has just about doubled every year since. Today's chips may have tens of thousands of transistors and other components, along with their electrical connections. Because of the simple raw materials and the production technology—a type of photolithography which permits easy pattern changes—the cost of chips has not risen as their possibilities have leaped forward. The price per integrated circuit function has actually fallen by an annual average of 27.5 percent. This may now level off, as chips grow more and more complex.

If all goes well, the microprocessor—a chip with many of the powers of a computer—will soon enter its fourth generation. It will then have the same word length as a large computer. It is in microprocessors, introduced in 1971, that the real economic future of communications and information lies. Already used to control innumerable devices and to link groups of devices, they are becoming capable of larger and larger chores. And, among other things, they power the toy industry. The two biggest microprocessor buyers in the world are the toymakers Milton Bradley and Mattel.

Microelectronics and Telephones Merge

The telephone system today scarcely resembles that of two decades ago. Using computers, microwave, fiber optics, and technologies for packeting information for maximum efficiency in transmission, the telephone is moving from narrowband analog transmission networks designed for voice to broad-band networks which carry voice, video, data, and many other types of signals. This is made possible through technology which converts print, voice, ordinary numbers, pictures, music—all analog forms of information—into digital form.

United States overseas message telephone services grew from $357 million in 1972 to $976 million in 1978. The satellite plays its role here. In 1970, transatlantic telephone calls used a satellite with a carrying capacity of 1200 telephone circuits. By 1979, the capacity of satellites had increased tenfold, and the cost of hiring a circuit had fallen to little more than a quarter of the 1960s price. Satellite traffic in the United States is well advanced toward use for direct business-to-business service using office roof antennas.[8]

An Arthur D. Little study projects that 523 million main telephone stations will be operating worldwide by 1991, and that telecommunications equipment markets worth more than $367 billion will spring up during the 1980–1990 period. This will nearly double that of the 1970s and will continue to increase at a steady pace. This study projected that by the end of 1980, for the first time, there would be more telephone stations in Europe than in North America. The Report says:[9] "Perhaps of even greater significance, by the end of 1980 we predict there will be more main stations installed in Asia than there were in North America in 1970."

The study estimates that in 1975, telecommunications concerns worldwide collected almost $88 billion in revenues, 45 percent of which was collected by North American common carriers. In 1980, projected operating revenues were expected to exceed $171 billion, and equipment markets to reach at least $51 billion.

Technology has made time and distance irrelevant, so that the most expensive part of the telephone system is now often the "local loop." Costs may be further cut by fiber optic transmission, which:[10] ". . . promise(s) to make it possible to transmit the contents of 40,000 books down a single glass fiber the width of a human hair in one hour."

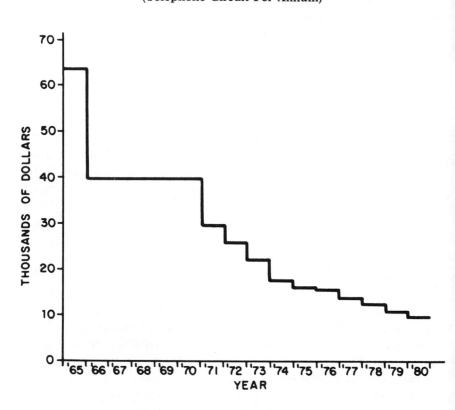

INTELSAT UTILIZATION CHARGES
(Telephone Circuit Per Annum)

Over the past fifteen years, costs on INTELSAT have
dropped dramatically. INTELSAT handles about two-
thirds of all transoceanic communications and links 131
of the world's countries and territories. (From INTEL-
SAT. Reprinted by permission.)

By 1984, New England will be linked to Washington, D.C.,
by a half-inch fiber optics telephone cable which will be able
to carry 40,000 conversations simultaneously. This replaces
a many times larger copper wire cable which carries 2800
conversations, and costs much more.[11] Fiber optics is a system
in which sound waves are converted to laser light waves for

transport through very clear glass threads. Not only can many more strands be incorporated in a "cable" than with copper wire, but each strand carries more signals, and light signals are faster than electric signals. Over time, Bell Telephone hopes to totally phase out electric circuits in favor of an integrated optical system for all phones. Fiber optics is expected to be especially useful in cities, where the highly efficient but small cable can fit into existing conduits, eliminating massive needs to dig. This same ability to fit existing conduits will serve it well over long distances.

There were six U.S.-European and two Canadian-European transatlantic telecommunications cables in use in 1980, and by 1983, there will be two more. Attempts to create a submarine fiber optics cable are underway, and it is hoped that this will be in place by 1988 or 1989.[12]

Enter the Satellites

Out of the U.S. space program developed in response to the Soviet Sputnik launch in 1957 have come communications satellites, satellites to gather weather data, satellites for sensing remotely the earth's resources, and, of course, military satellites.

Experiments with the passive reflecting satellite, Echo (1958–1960), and its successor, Telstar, demonstrated that, with a large earth station, a radio signal could be sent to a satellite several thousand miles out in space. It arrived in weakened condition, but with reamplification it could be rebroadcast to another earth station, thousands of miles from the first. Any two earth stations in sight of the same satellite could thus communicate with each other. COMSAT's Early Bird, or INTELSAT I, launched in 1965, had a total of 120 circuits and permitted communications between the East Coast USA and earth stations in Western Europe (one each in France and England at that time) and North Africa. Between 1966 and 1968, INTELSAT II, with 240 equivalent voice-grade circuits, was introduced, which covered the North and South

Atlantic and the continents of Africa and South America, and could be used as far east as Kuwait and as far west as Mexico City. The Pacific basin was also tied in. With INTELSAT III in 1969, a fully global system became operational and from that time forward, the capability of communicating television programming, teletype, telegraph, and telephone messages, and computer data traffic grew and grew.[13]

Efforts are now underway by Canada and Japan (using U.S.-developed technology) to develop domestic direct broadcasting by satellite TV (DBS-TV), which can be received from the satellite in small "dishes" by individual television viewers. In the United States, Satellite Television Corporation, a COMSAT subsidiary, has also applied for Federal Communications Commission permission to provide a service of this nature.

The LANDSAT satellite system, which is placed in polar orbits, measures, records, and sends to earth the reflection of electromagnetic energy—absorbed from the sun—from the surface of the globe. Since every object on earth has characteristic radio signatures, each can be individually identified. Ores and potential petroleum sources can be located. Grains, forests, and other agricultural products, even whether they are healthy or unhealthy, can be distinguished. The condition of coastal zones can be determined. This information is useful for agricultural purposes, land and crop inventory and management, management of water resources, mineral and petroleum exploration, and for the use of other scientific disciplines.

A Radiant View of Earth

Sensing, which is often assumed to be photographic although it is not, is done in four color bands—blue, green, and two infrareds. This sensing produces dots of varying shades of gray to represent the radio energy involved. Each dot now represents about an acre of ground or water. About 64 shades of gray can be distinguished. But equipment on LANDSAT IV will be able to refine this to about 120.[14]

Satellites developed for military uses, along with an array of ground-, sea-, and air-based sensing devices, are employed for national technical means of verification of such treaties as SALT and for peacekeeping, for instance in the Sinai between Egypt and Israel.

Interactive television, automated office equipment systems, smaller and better cameras, video discs and tapes, new recording devices—the list of new communications and information resources grows steadily. They are all tools, and they are there for our use. But only we can develop the ingenuity to make these tools work for us, and not vice versa.

Right now, all these innovations and new industries are running around freely, each doing its own thing. And that is excellent for youthful development. But, as with all youth, some sort of thought must be given to keeping them out of trouble, and guiding them toward a constructive and well-organized maturity.

Dynamics within the
U.S. Communications and
Information Resources Sector*

3

THERE are many facets to communications and information resources, and each is important as technologies grow and customs change. Each facet shifts under its own pressures. And when they join to form new patterns, it's a whole new ball game.

Fundamental Shifts

The first facet is the *conduit,* or the physical channel by which information travels. This may be a system like the postal system, or it may be a specific physical channel such as coaxial cable, satellites, or optical fibers. The second facet is the *content,* or the information the medium contains. Things like news, entertainment, advertising, and financial or other data

* The concepts discussed in this chapter are substantially based on the work done by Harvard's Program on Information Resources Policy, and especially on the work of Benjamin Compaine and John McLaughlin.[1]

are included here. The third facet is *format*, which is especially vulnerable to technological change. Format is the physical form of the display of the content: ink on paper, pictures on a video tube, sound from a speaker, magnetized information on computer tapes, punched cards, photocopied materials, or facsimile. A fourth facet is the *hardware*, or the machinery involved, which could be telephone sets, computers, microphones, typewriters, remote sensing equipment, or transistor radios.

The user—business or industry or government or the military or a private person—is not concerned with these facets so much individually as with how they all—the conduit, the content, the format, the hardware—fit together to get a given job done. And so a fifth facet is *function*. Is this broadcasting, publication, data transmission, message service, or what?

The obvious shift that can be seen taking place here is one of taste, or demand for content. Television, radio, and films have made inroads on reading. While television has captured much of radio's original audience, radio is itself expanding into new territory. Advertising follows the customer to whatever medium has the greatest power to attract. The shifts are also occurring in the types of data processing demanded and the types of telecommunications necessary.

As might be expected, there is a wholesale shift away from the clumsier, less efficient, and more expensive conduits, formats, and hardwares, toward more efficient and less expensive ones. Newsprint making is highly energy intensive and newspaper delivery is highly labor intensive, requiring 1.5 million people daily to haul papers and throw them on the customer's doorsteps. Newspapers are attempting to compensate by using many electronic techniques. The postal system, with its armies of letter carriers, is also highly labor intensive, and so is turning toward electronic mail. The U.S. banks still laboriously handle their checks, which now number 30 billion a year, but this is changing. Photocopying is quicker and cheaper than typing. Optical fibers are more efficient than copper wires. So it is easy to see which way the trend leads here.

But it is when these new types of content, format, conduit, and hardware start to fit together to do the job in almost entirely new ways that the big, fundamental changes start to take place.

Already in the old print media, lines were a little blurred. There were such questions as what constitutes a magazine vs. a book, when does a newsletter become a magazine, and so on. But in television, these lines are much less distinct. From what it sees on the screen, a TV audience doesn't know whether the show is being broadcast over the air or delivered by cable or is playing from a video cassette or a videotape. And the audience doesn't care (except in subscribing for service), any more than it cared whether what it read was called a book or a magazine or a newsletter. But the television broadcasters care, their suppliers care, and the agencies regulating the whole affair care. What format, what content, what conduit, and what hardware is involved is of supreme importance to those in the industry and their governmental guardians.

There are now 116 government agencies and departments whose job it is to regulate business in the United States. Twenty of these have sprung up since 1970. At least fifteen,* including some of the newest, now concern themselves with communications and information resources.[2] Their job grows more complex daily, and so does that of the communications and information resources industries.

Information Worlds Collide

Until a few years ago, telecommunications could be entirely differentiated from computers in a regulatory sense. IBM and other computer companies were free-wheeling competitive

* Postal Rate Commission, Interstate Commerce Commission, Civil Aeronautics Board, Federal Communications Commission, Federal Reserve Board, Comptroller of the Currency, Federal Deposit Insurance Corporation, Federal Home Loan Bank Board, Federal Savings and Loan Insurance Corporation, Securities and Exchange Commission, U.S. Postal Service (regulatory function), Federal Trade Commission, Department of Justice, Equal Employment Opportunity Commission, Occupational Safety and Health Administration, and Environmental Protection Agency.

private enterprises, with minimal regulation. Telecommunications was a regulated monopoly. But now, computers largely make up the central office of a telephone company. And now, telephones are used to transmit all sorts of computer data as well as voice. And now, satellites as well as cables are used to convey all these messages and data. And—this is the important part—these different functions fall into the bailiwicks of different people, and are subject to different regulatory mechanisms.

The problem now, in strictly technological terms, is that computing and communications can no longer be differentiated.* But the involved industries and the regulatory agencies are still vitally concerned about which is which. So are the world's Post, Telephone, and Telegraph Administrations (the PTTs). And the world over, all these different interests are engaged in a mighty struggle to hold onto what they consider to be their very own turf while moving onto the turf of others.

One point where battle lines are being drawn is over the telephone yellow pages. In 1979, Bell Telephone got $2.3 billion of its revenues from these pages. At the same time, the large American daily newspapers were getting 23 percent of their revenues from their classified ads. Each had its own audience because the yellow pages only came out once a year. But now the telephone system would like to use its new electronic technology to put the yellow page information on TV-like screens in the customer's home. This would save print costs and delivery costs and give the users great convenience. Moreover, the information would be constantly updated, and therefore come in direct competition with the classified ads.

Another point of complication is that very soon it will be possible to digitize *all* types of information, whether it is for the print media or the electronic media, or whether it is financial or corporate information, or whether it is a voice message or computer data or music or a picture. It can then all be transmitted, domestically or internationally, as zeros and ones,

---

* The merging of computers and communications is frequently called *compunications* by Americans and *télématique* by the French.[3]

and over the same lines. There will be no difference whatsoever and no way to distinguish between these information types while they are in transit. This is of concern to those people who would restrict one type of data and not another.

Within the print and electronic broadcast media, a legal confusion is arising due to territorial crossing. *Time* magazine and *The Wall Street Journal,* for instance, now use satellites to transmit copy to printing plants far from the point where the news is analyzed, written, and dummied up. The dividing line between the electronic and print media is therefore vanishing. Both are using the electromagnetic spectrum, which has important ramifications under present laws. By statute and interpretation of the First Amendment, the print media and the electronic media are treated radically differently. An update of the First Amendment interpretation seems absolutely indicated. But this is very, very tricky. The print media could just as easily end up restricted as the electronic media could end up freed.[4]

Confusions related to trade are also arising. Is a broadcast, or the advertising on it, a commodity? What is the value of a computer tape? Must customs be paid for the information contained in a stack of punched computer cards? Or are the cards—as has been jokingly proposed—just "used paper"?

Another domestic U.S. change which will eventually have enormous international implications is that communications and information companies, including the largest, like IBM, AT&T, and McGraw-Hill, are crossing lines. They are beginning to regard themselves as information industries, not as computer companies or telecommunications companies or publishers. It has been said that the railroads made the mistake of considering themselves in the railroad—not the transportation—business. There is a concerted effort to avoid this mistake in the communications and information area.

Industries Cross Over

Harvard investigators have "mapped" the U.S. domestic information business, using 80-odd products and services with facets ranging from conduit to content to show how the activities of twelve corporate bodies are rapidly shifting.[5]

An increasing proportion of AT&T's "plain old telephone service" is now processed and delivered around the world using computer-assisted techniques, which used to be the domain of IBM and others in the data processing industry. The division between clearly regulated telecommunications and unregulated data processing has thus blurred within the functions of computer switching and transmission facilities. The Federal Communications Commission, in its Computer Inquiries I and II, has therefore tried to separate out its regulatory telecommunications jurisdiction while opening up computer products and enhanced services (computer processing) to competition.[6]

IBM today is not just concerned with computers, but is involved in defense telecommunications systems, service bureaus, copiers, printers, and business forms. Satellite Business Systems—IBM's consortium with Aetna Life Insurance and COMSAT—has overcome its major legal hurdles and is now moving full speed ahead. IBM will get involved in common carrier types of activities, and will have dealings in telegraph, FM subcarriers, and satellites.

IBM and AT&T will thus cover just about the whole eighty items on the communications and information resources map. But they are not alone. Xerox has a goodly piece of the computer printing equipment, film, facsimile, mailing equipment, software, and time-sharing business. Xerox recently acquired Western Union International. RCA also has activities in the various territories: satellites, telephones, broadcasting, books and records, satellite equipment, antennas, TV sets and equipment, videotape and disc equipment, and defense telecommunications systems.

Publishing companies—the New York Times, the Washington Post, Time Inc., and others—have entered the direct mail, film, TV programming, news service, broadcast station, and paper industries. McGraw-Hill not only deals in magazines and books, but provides information services which are increasingly electronically delivered, and almost all computer

THE "INFORMATION BUSINESS"

SERVICES

PRODUCTS

CONDUIT →

← CONTENT →

U.S. MAIL
PARCEL SVCS
COURIER SVCS

OTHER DELIVERY SVCS

PRINTING CO'S
LIBRARIES

RETAILERS

NEWSSTANDS

TELEPHONE
TELEGRAPH
MAILGRAM
IRC'S

SCC'S
VAN'S
CABLE OPERATORS

MULTIPOINT DIST. SVCS

SATELLITE SVCS
FM SUBCARRIERS

PAGING SVCS

INDUSTRY NETWORKS

DEFENSE TELECOM SYSTEMS
SECURITY SVCS

BROADCAST NETWORKS
CABLE NETWORKS
BROADCAST STATIONS

TIME SHARING

NEWS SERVICES   FINANCIAL SVCS

DATA BASES
TELETEXT

SERVICE BUREAUS

ON-LINE DIRECTORIES

SOFTWARE SVCS

PROFESSIONAL SVCS

ADVERTISING SVCS

LOOSE-LEAF SVCS

DIRECTORIES

COMPUTERS

PABX'S

RADIOS
TV SETS
TELEPHONES
TERMINALS
PRINTERS
FACSIMILE
ATM'S
POS EQUIP
ANTENNAS
FIBER OPTICS
CALCULATORS

TELEPHONE SWITCHING EQUIP

MODEMS   CONCENTRATORS

MULTIPLEXERS

TEXT EDITING EQUIP

SOFTWARE PACKAGES

NEWSPAPERS

NEWSLETTERS

MAGAZINES

PRINTING AND
GRAPHICS EQUIP

COPIERS

CASH REGISTERS

INSTRUMENTS

TYPEWRITERS
DICTATION EQUIP
FILE CABINETS
PAPER

WORD PROCESSORS
PHONO'S, VTR'S, VIDEO DISC
MICROFILM   MICROFICHE
BUSINESS FORMS

COMMUNICATING WP'S

MASS STORAGE

SHOPPERS

AUDIO RECORDS
AND TAPES
VIDEO PROGRAMS

BOOKS

ATM — Automated Teller Machines
IRC — International Record Carrier
PABX — Private Automatic Branch Exchange
POS — Point-of-Sale

SCC — Specialized Common Carrier
VAN — Value Added Network
VTR — Video Tape Recorder
WP — Word Processor

The rapidly developing information business is centered on the computer as the main driving force. (From "Mapping the Information Business," John F. McLaughlin with Anne E. Birinyi, Program on Information Resources Policy, Harvard University, 1980. Copyright © 1980 by The President and Fellows of Harvard College. Reprinted by permission.)

organized and manipulated. And Dun and Bradstreet, which has been active in publications for years, has recently bought companies which will take it into data processing and information distribution.

Businesses not formerly concerned with communications and information are also getting into the act. Chase Manhattan, Citibank, and other financial institutions are offering time sharing, data bases, consulting services, and service bureaus. And EXXON Enterprises is heavily involving itself in a wide variety of electronics equipment.

"Will EXXON put a tiger in your TV set . . .?" asks one magazine article whimsically.[7] But *Business Week* predicts that EXXON's tiger will do no less than try to gobble up both IBM and Xerox! Over the years, EXXON has quietly bought up 15 small companies in the information area, which by the end of the 1980's:[8] ". . . could produce $10 billion to $15 billion in revenues." This could get EXXON as much as 10 percent of the total market for advanced office systems by the end of the 1980s, but their goal is said to be much more long term than that.

Big Bucks in Black Boxes

Within the automated office arena, a bigger business than data processing is predicted to be in place by the end of this decade. Administrative tasks, it is said, will be entirely changed by interlocking and interchangeable office machines powered by microprocessors. "Black boxes" which automatically route phone calls into the cheapest line available are already in use. Groups of small computers are being linked to high-capacity cables by microprocessors. Office files are being automated and converted to single systems. Altogether, the automated office business in the United States is said to be growing at a rate of close to 50 percent a year. EXXON has so far invested $500 million in EXXON Information Systems—ESI—(of which EXXON Enterprises is the parent), and is now making intelligent typewriters, microprocessors, text editors and display screens, voice response, voice input, and voice message systems, and semiconductor lasers for use in optical fiber communications networks. It will soon be coming out with a switching network to tie the whole thing together. EXXON was spending less than $47 million a year in 1979 on research and development for advanced office equipment, while Xerox spent $376 million and IBM $1.4 billion. But, says *Business Week*, EXXON has ". . . sales that approach the gross national product of Mexico . . ." ($84.8 billion) to back it up, and has just begun its challenge. If this continues, it is only a matter of time before ESI will enter the international marketplace.

Regarding regulations, the Harvard group says: "The current position and strategic movements of corporate bodies within the information business suggests that their future nature will invite regulatory conflict."

Regulatory Chaos

At this time, the Postal Rate Commission regulates the U.S. Postal Service, while the Interstate Commerce Commission regulates the United Parcel Service, and the Civil Aeronautics Board regulates air courier services. The Federal Communications Commission concerns itself with telecommunications, common carriers, broadcasting, cable, and many other services and products. The Postal Rate Commission and the Federal Communications Commission both claim rights to regulate electronic mail. Financial services may be regulated by the Federal Reserve Board, the Comptroller of the Currency, the Federal Deposit Insurance Corporation, the Federal Home Loan Bank Board, and the Federal Savings and Loan Insurance Corporation, as well as by multiple agencies of the state governments involved. The U.S. Postal Service (in its regulatory role), the Federal Trade Commission, and the Federal Communications Commission all have some power over advertising services. The Federal Reserve Board, by operating "Fed-Wire," gets into telecommunications, and the Federal Communications Commission controls the operation of radio

FUNCTIONAL REGULATION OF THE INFORMATION BUSINESS

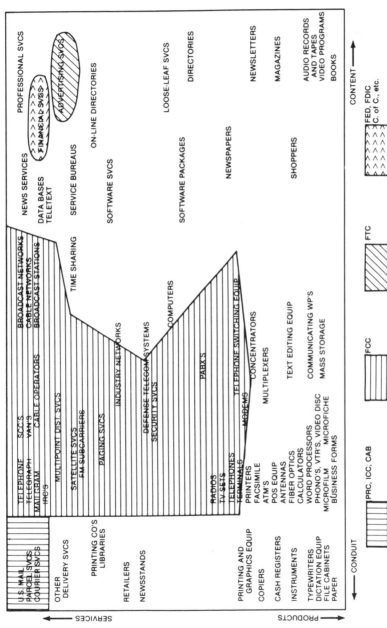

Just some of the regulators of the information business, which now number at least fifteen. (From "Mapping the Information Business," John F. McLaughlin with Anne E. Birinyi, Program on Information Resources Policy, Harvard University, 1980. Copyright © 1980 by The President and Fellows of Harvard College. Reprinted by permission.)

and television stations by newspaper publishers. Other regulatory bodies involved in the communications and information area are the Department of Justice, the Federal Trade Commission, the Equal Employment Opportunity Commission, the Occupational Safety and Health Administration, and the Environmental Protection Agency.

Some of the foregoing problems have been recognized in the United States by the executive branch, the Congress, and the Federal Communications Commission. Concerted efforts are being made to encourage competition in domestic telecommunications, to remove the artificial restraints between computers and telecommunications, and generally to attempt to "deregulate" the telecommunications industries. But this has by no means been accomplished.

The same sorts of confused regulatory jurisdictions, only worse, exist around the world, and each country has its own peculiar mix. To complicate matters more, foreign governments often both operate and regulate certain industries. The European PTTs are a case in point. When unresolved U.S. domestic regulatory problems cross borders and meet equally unresolved problems in other countries, businessmen and policymakers can expect fireworks. There have already been many preliminary bangs.

Communications and Information Dynamics within General U.S. Industry

4

As early as 1970, researchers found that about half of the U.S. labor force was working in communications and information-related jobs, and about half of U.S. labor income was derived from communications and information-related sources.[1] Figures approaching this amount are available for other advanced countries. This concept was and still is ridiculed by most of general industry, where the equivalent of the following is said: If half of everything derives from communications and information resources, then where do you fit in things like steel and cotton balls?

All major U.S. industries have installed computers and other communications and information devices. But most tend to consider them as mere administrative and clerical aids. There is a figure of about 2 or 2.5 percent which most major companies will cite as their communications and information-resources expenditures, regardless of how they actually use

U.S. OCCUPATIONS OVER THE LAST CENTURY

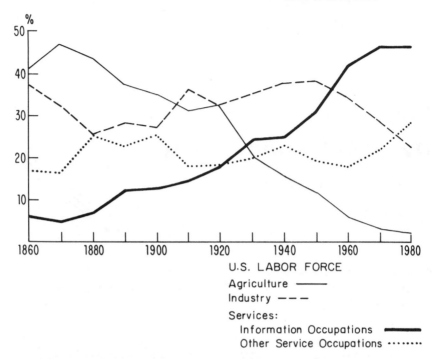

U.S. LABOR FORCE

Agriculture ———
Industry — — —
Services:
   Information Occupations ▬▬▬
   Other Service Occupations ⋯⋯⋯

While the percentage of jobs for farmers and industrial workers goes down, the percentage of jobs for information and other service workers is on the rise. (From Marc U. Porat, *The Information Economy: Definition and Measurement*, Vol. 1, U.S. Dept. of Commerce, Washington, D.C., May 1977. Reprinted by permission.)

them. The fact is that most companies do not have the foggiest notion of what they actually spend on communications and information, because they have never spent any time thinking about it.

Differentiation through Information

There are three general types of industry in the United States:

- Heavy industry and consumer products manufacturers.
- "Paper flow" industries, such as large banks, insurance companies, and financial institutions.
- Communications and information resources businesses, which deal in computers and communications equipment and services.

The first two of these will usually deny having anything whatsoever to do with communications and information resources. But a very curious phenomenon which questions this perception has been cropping up across industry lines.

There are, for instance, about ten major steel companies in the United States, of which Inland Steel is the sixth largest. It is, however, the third most profitable. This is partly because, in 1971, it had the foresight to install the sort of information-resources system which permitted it to find where it had put its ingots after it had made them, and to give its customers precise information on when, how, and where they would be delivered. In this way, the company saved a fortune on inventory, and more important, differentiated itself with its customers from its competitors.

Most U.S. companies, according to a consulting firm dealing with the Fortune 500, simply do not know, without a rather tedious and time-consuming search, where they have put their "ingots" or the precise details of their delivery.[2]

Dow Chemical was the first to do the same sort of thing in the chemical industry. Everybody in the industry had the same access to raw materials, and shipped a carload of whatever to wherever at roughly the same price. But Dow installed a system to give its customers detailed information, and thereby helped increase its share of the market.

In the banking business, all banks have approximately the same buildings, the same loan rates, the same products to offer. But Citibank differentiated itself from the rank and file. It spent $14 million on the information technology to put 24-hour self-service banking terminals in place. The other banks said that this was very foolish. But the best they could do to compete with Citibank was to stay open until five, reopen on Thursday evenings, or pay their help time-and-a-half on

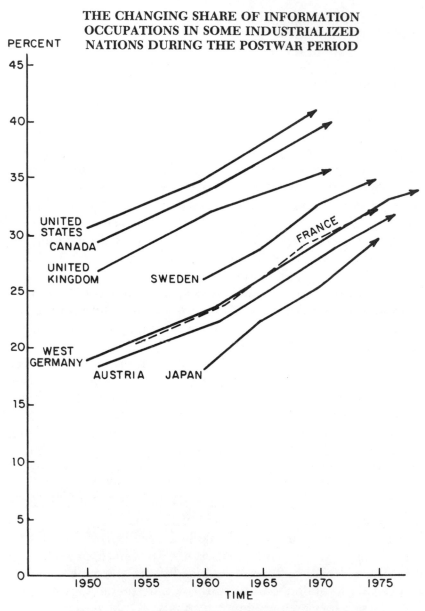

THE CHANGING SHARE OF INFORMATION
OCCUPATIONS IN SOME INDUSTRIALIZED
NATIONS DURING THE POSTWAR PERIOD

All the advanced countries are showing increases in information-related occupations. (Based on OECD document DSTI/ICCP/80.10, Paris, June 6, 1980.)

Saturdays (and listen to them gripe). Citibank picked up a much bigger share of the market, and provided more information than the teller could without using tellers. And the customers loved it. Citibank is said to have gained 2 percent of New York's banking business just for letting people punch out their own bank balances. The bank is rapidly getting its investment back.

Pan American Airlines was able to turn its badly troubled business around by the installation of sophisticated communications and information systems. They had not known where their spare planes were, or what the passenger loads were, or where their parts were located, or even which routes were most profitable. It is said that most American businesses do not know which of their lines are most profitable or do not know in time to make quick shifts.

More important, at Pan Am each managerial section had its own set of figures, which it used to promote its own set of ends. By installing an intricate communications and information system that made a single set of figures available to everyone, Pan Am:[3]

- Schedules its passengers and cargo instantly through a central processor in New Jersey, linked to 1500 terminals around the world.
- Links into all other major airlines.
- Knows where every airplane and part is at a given moment.
- Keeps every mechanic informed in every part of the world of what has been done or not done to a given plane.
- Provides weather information, constantly updated, to its terminals worldwide.
- Reschedules its flights for weather or other reasons to within 15 minutes of departure.
- Routes and fuels its planes individually to optimize fuel use and cost.
- Schedules crews on a worldwide basis, minimizing "synthetic" pay by tracking their hours by computer.
- Accounts for worldwide profits and losses as each 24-hour period passes and makes adjustments accordingly.

The U.S. railroad industry has recently discovered computers, and is fascinated by the fact that one can actually know where a freight car is, when it might arrive, and what might be on it.[4] This had all been handled by mail, and the information they were getting was where the car had been a few days before, and the information usually arrived a few days after the car itself. While Pan Am punched a computer terminal for instant data on space availability, railroad personnel called one of their several hundred stations and sat on "hold" waiting for an answer. This state of affairs certainly couldn't have helped the railroad in competition for freight and passenger traffic. They say they are already getting their investment in communications equipment back.

Heavy industry not only is using communications and information devices to differentiate itself from its competitors and to shape its management but has also installed a variety of devices to control intricate production phases of actual products. One instance cited has been the steel industry. The controlled processes for one hot-strip mill, which produces sheet steel for auto bodies, household appliances, and other products, is said to operate thus:[5] The steel comes into the mill in foot-thick red hot slabs, which must be flattened by a sequence of rollers to a thickness of .01 inch or less. During this process, the temperature must be absolutely controlled— not too hot, not too cold. Because the slab gets longer as it gets thinner, each succeeding set of rollers must run faster and faster, to speeds reaching 35 miles per hour. Any foulup in any part of the operation means costly re-do's, mill shutdowns, and many lesser problems. Reception of the new slab, start-up of the process, regulation of gap width of each roller set (easily contorted by heat), regulation of speed of each roller set, temperature regulation of the slabs to synchronize with rolling time, correction of temperature at any step in the process, and a variety of sensor tasks for many types of error correction are all accomplished by multiple electronic communications and information devices. In addition, the information gained and recorded is used to analyze the mill's performance on a continuing and overall basis.

In October 1980, an article appeared in *Transnational Data Report*, entitled "Ford Saves $180M with Transnational Design Net," and included the following quote:[6]

Ford Motor Company claims to have saved at least $180 million by pooling its international design resources for the new project Erika small car, sold in Europe as the Escort. One of the key aids to using an international team was "a transnational computer network" which has linked design teams in Europe and the United States . . . .

Speedy Dollars and Speedier Cards

The number of checks written in the United States has been climbing 7 percent a year. By 1979, this had reached 30 billion items annually and is expected to double within the next decade. Presently, 85 percent of all money in the United States flows in some way through electronic networks—through clearinghouses, bank-to-bank transfers, and through corporate paycheck systems. But, although such electronic processes are helpful, banks are actively looking for better ways to handle this runaway paper flow. The future seems to be toward total electronic processing.[7]

The bank credit card industry, and Visa specifically, uses an electronic payment system for card transactions which eliminates the transfer of paper between senders. Visa provides two principal services to 12,000 participating financial institutions worldwide: *authorization,* and a sales ticket clearing mechanism called *interchange.*

In December 1978, during a peak hour, over 30,000 transactions—authorization requests for individual customer purchases—took place. Response time dropped from five minutes in 1973 to five seconds by 1978. For computer interface sites, this response time is as low as two seconds.

The total transactions by Visa grew from 450 million in 1974 to about a billion in 1978. Its sales figures rose to $38 billion in 1979, up 30 percent from 1978. Of this amount, about $10 billion were international. Visa consolidated its international operations in 1974, and now operates in 120 countries. It has electronic linkages for authorization in the United Kingdom, France, Spain, Italy, and Canada, using 2400- and 9600-bits-per-second telephone lines, and such linkage for other European countries and other areas of the world is now being developed. Visa had 74 million of the total 155 million plastic bank card customers in 1978, for which there were a total of 1.7 billion transactions and a sales volume of $58 billion.[8] The number of Visa cardholders had risen to 84.1 million by 1979.

In short, at whatever U.S. business or industry one cares to look today, the chances are good of finding communications and information resources playing a major if unheralded role.

Information as Hero

The worldwide information system of U.S. oil companies—put in place originally to handle the routine day-to-day scheduling of tankers and inventories—was put to emergency use during the 1973 oil crisis, and may well have saved the industrialized world from disaster at that time. The same system, by now more finely tuned to deal with sudden supply fluctuation, minimized the trauma brought about by events in Iran. In the same vein, it is said that the availability of communications and information resources, which permitted quick measures to be taken by numerous people, may have saved the stock market from at least chaos during the March 1980 silver market debacle. An editorial entitled "Saved by (Ma) Bell?" had this to say:[9]

It was a close call, that silver market dustup of March 27. For a while, ominous bulletins from Wall Street told of calls for more margin, of a stampede by speculators to sell stock, of brokerage firms that were straining to unload portfolios. Silver prices plummeted more than 50% on that day. And yet, before the trading day ended, much of the damage had been isolated and contained. The very next day, the market rebounded.

A domino effect did not ripple through the economy. Why?

It had to be more than plain luck. Along with regulatory safe-guards that were built in after the Great Crash of 1929, this time we had modern communications going for us. As telephones, satellite communications, computers and video display facilities fed information from and to the trading areas, those empowered to make decisions could act swiftly. And the brakes held.

As brokers, traders, regulators and the other watchdog groups now set out to learn lessons from that Thursday silver trauma, they should remember something that marketing people found out long ago: A communications system that is technologically up to the minute is worth its weight in gold. Or silver.

True, technology can also foster speculative excess, but it's good to have it at work to help bail us out when trouble occurs. There is no substitute for good communications for gathering and disseminating information that is needed to make decisions. And fast is best.

A study of eleven major U.S. multinationals with combined revenues of $83.5 billion in 1978 found them to use international data communications routinely in at least the following ways. Financial institutions and computer vendors and service vendors were not included in this group:[10]

- For the production, planning, and coordination of manufacturing schedules, the coordination of assembly of components manufactured in separate areas at one point (to effect economies of scale), the tracking and transfer of widely scattered expert personnel, major equipment, parts, and materials for use at worldwide sites.
- For collecting, processing, and submitting to headquarters financial, statistical, and other management data.
- For preparing software, often at headquarters, for regional distribution, and for its transmission.
- For recording and processing accounts receivable, order files, vendor information, and resource locations.
- For internal message networks, within and between subsidiaries and headquarters. This includes voice, facsimile, and so on.
- For collecting, processing, and recording health systems information, reservations systems (airlines and credit systems data, etc.).

(Most payroll, personnel files, and personnel schedules are handled at the local level and are not routinely processed internationally.)
• Some companies also have central major complex engineering systems for mathematical modeling, structural analysis, and other tasks, which are then transmitted to and shared in regional areas.

It is clear that modern international business and trade, which are worth more than $1 trillion a year, could not take place without modern communications and information resources. But despite this fact, there are almost no statistics available on the magnitude of information exchanged, the uses to which information is put, or on its dollar value. The Department of Commerce has a couple of sets of figures on overall international commercial interests in the information area, and the U.S. government reports consistently quote these. They show earnings for the information industry for 1975 of nearly $1 billion, and indicate that this is growing at a yearly rate of 15 to 25 percent. Not only are these figures hopelessly out of date, but they do not include any figures for general industry. Since communications and information resources are so intimately intertwined with the total operations of corporations, any parts would be difficult to identify with precision. But since they obviously play an important role in the daily business of these general industries, the largest proportion of the earnings for international communications and information-related activities must be assumed to be missing altogether.

The World Picks Up the Economic Challenge

5

WHILE the United States enjoys a head start in the communications and information resources area, and a positive balance of trade in high electronics, it should not believe that the rest of the world is standing idly by.*

Governments of other developed nations have, indeed, been quicker to recognize the revolutionary nature of these new knowledge-based technologies, products, and techiques than has the United States. They refer to the coming of a "second industrial revolution" based on these fields, and they are determined to play an active part. These new technologies, they believe, are absolutely vital to their future economic, security, and national sovereignty interests. They intend, therefore, to resist dependence on the United States in the communications and information area, or at least to keep that dependence to an absolute minimum. To do so, they are simultaneously bettering their own positions, while at the same

---

* The Communist countries do not at this time represent a competitive *economic* force in the communications and information area.

time attempting, as much as possible, to thwart U.S. access to international markets.

International Conflicts

The hottest international battles thus far center around the computer, data processing, microprocessors, and chips. Space and other electronic technologies are also becoming conflict areas.

United States revenues from its semiconductor and electronic devices industry are so far only about $6 billion a year. But other nations know very well that this figure is growing. And they also know that U.S. products worth more than $200 billion a year are incorporating advanced electronic components at a daily increasing rate.[1] The Germans are fully aware that their own important machine tool export trade is steadily growing more dependent on access to these components.

Whether the United States can be counted on as a dependable supplier of vital electronic products is much on the minds of some nations. The French recall that in the 1960s, the United States refused them advanced computers on nonproliferation grounds. South Africa, with a rapidly expanding data processing industry, was forced to step up its domestic computer industry in 1978 because the United States banned computer shipments there on grounds of human rights.[2] The United States also denies a host of computer information products to different countries for strategic reasons. The U.S. presidential threat in spring 1980 to deny Iran access to international communications systems, including INTELSAT, has done nothing to increase confidence in this area.

The 1977 Japanese *Computer White Paper* puts the nation's attitude toward computers—which is typical for most countries—this way:[3]

For Japan, the importance of the computer industry is two-fold. It is in itself a fundamental industry of a type which is knowledge-intensive and resource and energy-saving, and it is furthermore a strategic industry which contributes to the realization of a more sophisticated industrial structure.

In France, the electronic data processing industry has been elevated to the rank of a societal issue. It is said to be:[4] "The source of all evil and possibly all good."

As in Japan, in France this industry is seen as a sector vital to the improvement of productivity of all areas of the economy. France has also recognized the strategic importance of the electronic data processing industry, and its government has decided—with the apparent approval of the trade unions—to actively encourage data processing to improve productivity, although it fears that this may lead to some structural unemployment.

A substantial portion of the Simon Nora report to the President of France in 1978 concerned itself with these problems, and especially the problem of American dominance:[5]

Since the appearance of the first computers, data processing has become a strategic sector in most countries; conscious of the specificity of its raw material—data—States quickly became interested in this industry. In fact, since 1945 few areas except the atom have received such scrutinizing attention from governments: this vigilance was the expression of the will to limit American domination, even stronger here than in any other domain.

France has spent 200 billion francs between 1974 and 1980 to modernize its outdated telephone system. Paris has nine new telephone exchanges, 7 million kilometers of new cables, and 60,000 new chrome and glass telephone booths. France is planning to eliminate telephone directories by the end of the 1980s and to deliver the same information through televisionlike devices provided to subscribers free. Whether this ambitious plan will actually succeed in that time frame is open to question. But in any case, this is the wave of the future.

Other Europeans and the Japanese are very conscious of the dominance, or at least the major influence, of American computer industries in individual countries and regions. In Europe, IBM alone held 52 percent of the market in 1977. In Germany, this was 58 percent, and in France, 50 percent. In Japan, IBM currently has about 30 percent of the market, and contributes greatly to Japan's exports in the computer field. In fiscal year 1978, IBM's revenues in Japan were estimated at $1.23 billion, and exports from Japan represented about 15 percent of IBM-Japan's revenues.[6]

What Other Countries Are Doing

The governments of most industrialized nations have responded to the U.S. challenge in electronics by taking a major interest in the subject. This is especially true in France and Japan. Special plans have been drawn up, partnerships created between government and industry, and government money poured into a variety of supporting industries. Historically, the most famous of these plans was DeGaulle's controversial Plan Calcul in the 1960s. France has continued and intensified this effort to the present time. Japan now has a major government-industry partnership, which is moving ahead vigorously and quite successfully. It is making Japan a serious competitor in the United States in the electronics field, and to a lesser extent, in computers. There are complaints by U.S. microprocessor makers that the Japanese are getting ahead on the more sophisticated chips because under the commercial system in which they work, they do not depend so heavily on recouping their investments swiftly.

Germany and the United Kingdom have also supported their industries by various means. "Germany has no intention of remaining the captive market of U.S. computer systems manufacturers that it has been for more than 25 years . . ." is the way one American observer puts it.

Siemens has joined forces with the Japanese firm Fujitsu in a major effort to further reduce IBM's market share in Germany. That share had already been reduced from 72 percent in 1965 to a still healthy chunk of 58 percent in 1977.

In addition to sizable industrial investment, the German government provided about $230 million for research and development projects in its data processing industry from 1975 to 1979.[7]

The United Kingdom has had a long and troubled history of government support for its computer industry, which has ranged from direct subsidies to acting as purchasing agent for its products, to a quasi "hands-off" policy. After many ups and downs, a quite successful computer company—ICL—has evolved, which in 1979 had total sales of $1 billion, with $74 million in profits. But by 1981 it was again in trouble and had to seek assistance from the Japanese. The benefits, if any, of government policy for this industry are unclear.[8]

In 1979, the United Kingdom embarked on a major effort to develop British microelectronics production capabilities and to foster the use of microelectronics in many branches of British industry. If all the funds called for are provided, this subsidy will amount to about $800 million over a three-year period. This strategy is based partly on the cooperation of U.K.-based American industry, and on the assumption that American firms can be induced to provide some of the needed technology.

The French perception of some nations' approaches to the U.S. communications and information challenge goes like this:[9]

Japan set out to gather the necessary technological knowledge for the manufacture of computers. It then closed itself off to all outside meddling, setting up a Draconian protectionism. Guaranteeing outlets for its data processing industry, it based its growth and exporting capacity on mass production.

Germany, for its part, accepted American predominance right from the start. Little by little, once the basic technology had been acquired, it set about "Germanizing" the products: this is a policy it has followed in other domains, such as the nuclear. It was thus able to forge a solid industry, oriented upon export battlements.

Great Britain has followed a diversified policy: support of a national builder constituted an element of overall action in which the development of applications, training of users and links with telecommunications held eminent positions.

Concerns are also being voiced by Canada, which, after a good start, is experiencing a growing negative trade balance in the electronics and computer area. Canadian government reports call for "Buy Canada" policies and for design standards that will facilitate adoption of Canadian technology.[10] But at the same time, Canada's Northern Telecom is becoming a formidable competitor to Western Electric in the United States. This company is quietly expanding in the United States, and made 40 percent of its total sales there in 1979.

A summary of a study of overall U.S.-Canadian communications and information relations is included in Chapter 16 of this book.

Market Inroads and Protectionism

The European Economic Commission has gotten into the act with a new program aimed at helping the emerging European telematics (telecommunications, computer, microchip, and databank) industries to catch up with the Americans and the Japanese. The latter are also rapidly penetrating the European market.

A major staff report to the Commission (the Davignon report) says:[11]

At present, between a quarter and a third of the world market for telematics is in Europe. EEC companies have got 30 percent of the world market for telecommunications, 16 percent for computers and software, and 10 percent for electronic components and chips. The commission predicts rapid growth for all three, led by components. It expects the world components market, worth $2.7 billion a year at present, to be worth $36 billion by the late 1980's.

The report adds that in the crucial microelectronics component sector, Europe still imports more than 80 percent of its integrated circuits. This situation prevails, notwithstanding major individual national efforts for the past two decades. The report (quite rightly) points out: ". . . Europe has so far failed to mobilize its major asset, continental scale."

And the Commission recommends the taking of a series of measures calculated to see Europe capture one-third of the world's telematics market by 1990.

Among the more advanced developing nations, Brazil has adopted a policy for protecting the "formation phase" of its information sector. If Brazil's policies are successful, they can be expected to be emulated by other countries. The market for minicomputers has now been closed for more than two years to U.S. and other foreign vendors, and the law requires control of the industry by Brazilian nationals. It is expected that similar restrictions will be imposed on medium-scale systems as well. The stakes are quite high in the fast-expanding Brazilian computer market, which is estimated to be growing at an annual rate of 25–30 percent, about double the annual worldwide computer industry growth rate of 15 percent.[12]

At the beginning of 1979, U.S. concerns had 67 percent of the $6.2-billion world market of chips, while Japan had 16 percent and the Europeans, 10. This situation is now being rather successfully challenged by Europe and Japan. They have accomplished this by investing in research and development resources, and by producing a high-quality product in large quantities in an expanding market where there is a substantial shortage. Japan had 40 percent of the $589-million U.S. market for 16K chips in 1980 and is also making deep inroads into the U.S. chip market in Europe. Some of Japan's most recent technology in this area may lead to their even bigger success.

Communications and information developments in Japan are rapid and sophisticated. The difficult ideographs which make up the Japanese and other oriental languages have given the Japanese a major incentive to develop highly advanced facsimile and pattern-recognition devices. The resulting equipment can therefore handle the relatively simple English and various European languages much more easily than can Western equipment. It is the old "necessity is the mother of invention" principle at work, and it has put Japan way out ahead. Japan is also way out ahead in robots, with an estimated

10,000 in use in 1979, compared to 3000 in the United States and 850 in West Germany.[13]

High Tech Companies Leave Home

Both Japanese and European firms are buying up U.S. technologies and companies as fast as they can get their hands on them.[14] Thomson-CSF is buying Motorola's current chip technology and has know-how agreements with Motorola, which has operated a semiconductor plant in Toulouse since 1967. St.-Gobain–Pont-à-Mousson has a 51 percent interest in a joint venture with National Semiconductor in Aix-en-Provence. Matra, the French missile specialists, and Harris Corporation have a joint venture with Harris as a minority partner at Nantes. Schlumberger, a French mining and oil-field-services company, has bought Fairchild Camera. These U.S.-French joint ventures are receiving substantial French government aid. For instance, the Matra-Harris plant, worth $40 million, is said to be receiving $27.5 million in French state aid, and the St.-Gobain–National Semiconductor plant is receiving $22.9 million.

Philips, which already had a great deal of in-house expertise, bought the U.S. firm Signetics in 1975. Philips, which estimates that 52 percent of the world's chip production is now concentrated in sixteen major companies, claims to be the second largest chip maker after Texas Instruments.

Similarly, Japanese firms have acquired or have concluded major know-how or marketing agreements with American firms. For instance, TRW has established a joint company with Fujitsu, and Nippon Electric Company has bought out Electronic Arrays in California.

Many U.S. firms have now linked up with foreign enterprises. One reason for these shifts is that research and development for chip technology, until now quite cheap, is growing more expensive as the chips get more complex. Small businesses don't have sufficient resources, and large ones don't want to divert their capital to these activities.

DIVIDING THE WORLD'S MARKET FOR
MICROCHIPS

Companies Ranked By Percent of World Market Share	United States	Europe	Japan
More than 10%	Texas Instruments IBM		
Five to 10%	National Semiconductor Motorola Intel	Philips	
Two to 5%	Fairchild Camera Western Electric Mostek RCA	Siemens	Hitachi Toshiba N.E.C.
One to 2%	Hewlett-Packard Harris General Instruments Rockwell I.T.T.	Thomson-C.S.F.	Mitsubishi Fujitsu
Total Share	67%	10%	15%

United States dominance in the world microchip market
is being challenged. (Based on a chart from "Europe
Joins Microchip World," *New York Times*, January 29,
1980. Data are 1979 Philips estimates. Copyright ©
1980 by the New York Times Company. Reprinted by
permission.)

Developing Interest by the Developing World

While Western Europe and Japan have picked up the communications and information challenge and are competing
actively with the United States, there are grave questions as
to whether these highly advanced technologies are open to
the developing world. The third world, which sees itself as
having been excluded from industrialization, now feels it lacks
the means for entering the new communications and informa-
tion-service economy.

However, as the application of semiconductor technology
spreads to more and more products, developing nations will
try to take advantage of their abundant labor supply and low

wage rates. Indeed, through the operations of several multinational corporations, an increasing amount of production of
microprocessors, microelectronic products, and electronic
consumer goods has been carried out over the last ten years.
Such countries as Taiwan, Korea, Thailand, the Philippines,
Malaysia, Singapore, Hong Kong, and Indonesia have been
especially active. In some cases they have reached the third
or fourth technological level. And Singapore, for instance, has
a rather impressive software capability.[15]

The end result of all this worldwide activity will undoubtedly mean fiercer competition for the United States. But, in
the broader context of U.S. foreign policy and international
security aims, is that bad? Other countries are bound to capture larger market shares for existing products. The question
is whether the United States will continue to come up with
new products which can capture a share big enough long
enough to recoup R&D and plant investments. The real threat
to the United States is not the growing market share of other
countries, but the possibility that some country may leapfrog
U.S. technology and capture a large market for a product
the United States cannot offer. This is really what happened
in the subcompact automobile market.[16]

Regulatory Activities in Communications and Information Competition

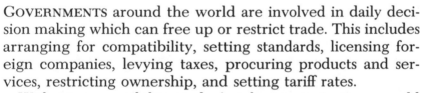

6

GOVERNMENTS around the world are involved in daily decision making which can free up or restrict trade. This includes arranging for compatibility, setting standards, licensing foreign companies, levying taxes, procuring products and services, restricting ownership, and setting tariff rates.

Without compatibility, today's telecommunications would be impossible. In the nineteenth century, when different systems resided within each national border, international communications by telephone and telegraph virtually did not exist. Early on, precursor organizations of the International Telecommunication Union were established to make arrangements to permit international message flow. And there is a similar need today for international standardization of interconnections between computer and telecommunications networks. The philosophy of the computer industry, which works with proprietary standards to enhance each participant's position in the marketplace, must be merged with the telecommunications philosophy, which works with nonproprietary and published standards.

Trade Weapons

But, while compatibility is essential for orderly world trade, for economies of scale in manufacturing, and for providing immense benefits in effectiveness, convenience, and reduced consumer prices, standards can serve as effective trade-war weapons. That is, they can be used to give advantages to particular products or services to the detriment of others. Conflicting objectives are thus being expressed in a variety of forums and countries regarding communications and information resources. The European nations are attempting to make data communications technology based on European standards mandatory. In addition to its laudable objectives, this is believed to also be an effort aimed at reducing the competitiveness of American companies in Europe. The Nora Report is, in fact, quite frank about this.

Licensing of foreign businesses is another way to either smooth the path or erect barriers in the way of international trade. The foreign-owned company may be treated with the same considerations and restraints as its national counterparts. On the other hand, the licensing authority may choose to:

- Refuse to issue a license to a potential foreign competitor.
- Set up all kinds of conditions which make the foreign company less competitive.
- Let the licensing procedure drag on and on.

Governments show remarkable inventiveness in the licensing area, and the list of potential obstacles is long.

In the communications and information sector, the cost of doing business, as in all other industries, determines competitiveness. In the case of telecommunications and computer data transmission, the PTTs have a triple weapon. They provide the services, regulate them, and also set the rates. This can be likened to giving American Telephone and Telegraph

(AT&T) the regulatory and rate-setting powers of the Federal Communications Commission (FCC) and the policy-making powers of the National Telecommunications and Information Administration (NTIA). As direct competitors to U.S. companies, the PTTs would like to use these rates to their own advantage. United States companies, for instance, have the technology to push a tremendous amount of information through circuits designed for a single telephone call. To maintain their own revenue base—which, in some countries, among other things, must subsidize the postal system—the PTTs want to use volume-sensitive pricing instead of flat-rate pricing. That is, they could penalize the American companies by charging for the actual volume used. A proposal to this effect is now before the CCITT.*

The same sorts of questions arise over the use of private lines vs. public networks. Large U.S.-owned multinationals find it much more economical to lease lines, which they can then employ as they like. The PTTs would like to force them to use the more expensive public network systems, since they feel private line use is too competitive for their telex and public switched telephone network (PSTN). American companies claim that public network use would drive the cost of international data communications up as much as tenfold. They also question whether the PTTs could match the reliability, security, service, and support now available with private line use.

While the PTTs have certain economic objectives, it should be noted that they play an even more important role as guardians of state interests in national telecommunications. In many European countries, telecommunications is a symbol of national sovereignty, in the same sense as roads, waterways, and other public utilities.

Government procurement is an important aspect of any government's effort to increase national competitiveness in high technology products and services. It has, in fact, been

* Consultative Committee for International Telephone and Telegraph of the International Telecommunication Union (ITU).

estimated that from 25 to 40 percent of the Gross National Product (GNP) of most countries passes through public budgets.[1] Discrimination against foreign products by government purchasing officials can, therefore, create an immense barrier in world trade.

In 1976, a European Economic Commission directive on public supply contracts, aimed at liberalizing government procurement from member country firms, granted a specific two-year exception for telecommunications services. This meant that national laws and policies could continue to determine telecommunications contract awards by the government for that period only. However, this exception was still in effect at the beginning of 1979.[2]

The U.S. government procurement code calls for open procedures in the bidding for and contract award process, and it is the U.S. goal that the code implementing the decisions of the Multilateral Trade Negotiations (MTN) of its major trading partners—the European Community nations, Japan, and the less developed countries—adopt the same procedures. United States companies hope services as well as products will be included in future codes. The United States is presently attempting, in the Trade Committee of OECD* and in GATT,† to negotiate less discriminatory national practices, not just in government procurement for the service industries, but across the board.

Obsolete Regulations, Out-of-Date Laws

In much of the world, telecommunications, including broadcasting, is considered so much a part of the power of the state that it is government owned and operated. It is not, therefore, surprising that in those few instances where private ownership is permitted, such ownership is restricted to a country's own nationals. Even the United States, which has few restrictions on foreign ownership in general, has severe pro-

* Organization for Economic Cooperation and Development.
† General Agreement on Tariffs and Trade.

hibitions on foreign ownership in the broadcasting industry. But some of these concepts are now being extended into the data communications area and into cable television. Storm clouds are also appearing in the new area of interactive television, where extension is also possible. Barriers are being created to U.S. data networks in Mexico and to U.S. ownership of cable television in Canada. This latter is a one-way street, since Canada has extensive, and rapidly expanding, cable TV ownership in the United States.[3]

A major problem here is that institutions, regulatory mechanisms, and laws have failed to keep pace—have not even begun to keep pace—with the rapid developments in communications and information resources. In the absence of more respectable devices, many countries are using some or all of these unsatisfactory techniques. Less than straightforward arguments and propositions are cropping up as countries try to turn the advantage to their own economy. This is, in principle, no different from the prevailing situation in commodities and other trade areas. What is different is that there are special political, social, and sovereignty features to the communications and information trade which are not commonly understood by trade negotiators or other decision makers, who find the environment surrounding these features foreign to their concepts.

The task of world leaders is rather complex:[4] On the one hand to become aware of these situations, understand what is bringing them about, and try to keep undesirable activities at a reasonable level; on the other hand to refrain from setting standards too soon and too rigidly. While definitive standards, regulatory techniques, and laws will inevitably be necessary, they should not be concretized at too early a stage, for this might well stifle further technological invention and innovation. There is no long-term advantage to any nation to be locked into standards which become obsolete. More satisfactory temporary arrangements for both domestic and international use should be worked out until the technologies reach a certain maturity and equilibrium.

The Changing Role of the Media in International Affairs

7

WHILE the communications and information industries and their contributions to general industry are enormously important in domestic and world affairs, it is the media and related information which strike at the greatest sensitivities of nations. Books, newspapers, magazines, television and radio programming, films, records, advertising—and even scientific data bases and technological know-how—all embody a cultural content which can in no way be politically inert. Economically, it is often more feasible for countries to buy U.S. films, television programming, and magazines than it is to produce these materials at home. It is also cheaper in many instances to rely on Western or U.S. news-gathering resources than it is to provide national ones. But new U.S. technological possibilities for media access to almost any part of the world, coupled with a vast increase in trade in media products internationally, are intensifying the distrust nations almost invariably feel when the culture of a foreign nation crosses their borders.

**EXPORTS OF U.S.-MADE FILMS AND SERIALS
FOR TELEVISION**

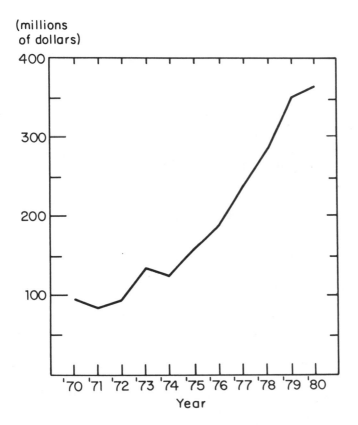

United States film and TV program exports provide
cheap entertainment for the world and give the United
States a positive balance of trade. But this is not without
cultural fallout. (Based on a chart from "Exports of
American-Made Television Movies," *New York Times*,
January 29, 1980. Copyright © 1980 by the New York
Times Company. Reprinted by permission.)

Despite national fears for sovereignty and resentment over
what they consider U.S. "cultural invasion," or "cultural imperialism," American television shows are bought and shown
all over the world, including the Soviet Union. This is because

people everywhere are demanding that their television screens be filled with programs for their entertainment. But to produce a show of U.S. prime-time quality—the quality of show people everywhere want to see—costs a great deal of money. One study indicates that the U.S. networks pay from $200,000 to $250,000 for a half-hour taped show. For a one-hour show, they may pay from $550,000 to $650,000. And for a made-for-TV two-hour movie, they may pay $1.5 to $2 million.[1] But these prices, shocking as they are, cover no more than 75 percent of production costs, and the gap between production costs and payments is rapidly widening.

Eventually, other U.S. domestic sales bring in money, but these sales must come after network use. Foreign sales, however, can be made simultaneously. So just to get back their production costs, the U.S. television industry tries to make up 10 to 20 percent abroad. The industry thus sells programming to other countries for prices ranging anywhere from $60 to a few thousand dollars. The U.S. companies can then finance the next shows' production and other countries can meet their television needs very cheaply. But what they are meeting them with is American programming, designed for American audiences, and carrying with it the American culture. The same sort of thing is true for American magazines, newspapers, records, and books.

U.S. films are also world favorites, for many of the same reasons, in both the industrialized and the developing world. In the middle of the 1970s, the U.S. film industry revenues from sales abroad were between $700 and $800 million, and at that time, the film industry gave the United States a positive balance of payments of $400 million.[2]

The presence of U.S. media in other countries is not a new phenomenon, and certainly it is not, as has been alleged, a "conspiracy" between the U.S. and Western governments and their media, publishing, and film industries. In quantitative terms, this pervasiveness of U.S. news has become especially noticeable since World War II, and has grown along with the overall international U.S. economic, military, and political presence. William Read, in his *America's Mass Media Merchants*, persuasively demonstrates that the phenomenon itself has existed at least since the 1920s.[3] He shows that, while the United States suffered from international isolationism at that time, U.S. motion picture companies and both AP and UP were internationally active. United States film makers were then already producing an estimated 90 percent of the movies shown abroad. By 1939, the United Press was directly serving 486 newspapers in 52 foreign countries, says Read.

Nor, despite its commitment to freedom of information, has the U.S. government always been happy with its domestic film industry, its press, or its TV. The film industry was severely criticized for:[4] ". . . handing over victory in the world's ideological struggle to the Kremlin on a celluloid platter." And from the cold war to Vietnam to the U.S. civil rights disorders to Tehran, there have been U.S. government accusations that the U.S. media distort the vision of America in the minds of the world. Voice of America, the U.S. government-owned and -operated broadcasting service, is mandated by statute to present only "objective" news. It broadcasts in 35 languages, through 123 stations, and claims to reach about 25 million people daily, and as many as 80 million during international crises. The United States is, of course, not the only country with active international media. *The Economist* and *Paris Match* are chosen alongside *Time* and *Newsweek* by the elite and upper classes all over the world.[5] The BBC also transmits in 39 languages besides English and broadcasts around the clock with its English World Service. Debates are in progress in Western Europe over the possible damage to the political structure of nations by TV broadcasts coming from many countries other than the United States. West Germany is worrying about Luxembourg's broadcasting television shows freely into its country, for instance, and France is expressing similar fears. There are many other examples, and all are aggravated by the future possibility of direct broadcasting by satellite (DBS-TV). But it is the inundation by American materials in newspapers, magazines, books, films, records, and television shows—

now being accelerated by the aid of new technologies—which is causing the greatest international resentment and concern.

Consider the case of Canada, for instance, where four out of five hours of English-language television watched by Canadian school children is programming of U.S. origin.[6] Or West Germany, where every second movie ticket sold is for an American-made film.[7] This cannot but be disturbing, and the same sort of problem is now present to some degree in many parts of the world. As a result, various types of limitations on U.S. content and access to news are cropping up worldwide. These vary in kind and quality from outright censorship and obstruction to limitations on content to a demand for a New World Information Order. Nor are these limitations confined to the communist countries or to the developing countries or to countries with dictatorships. Such stalwart democracies as the United Kingdom, Australia, and the aforementioned Canada have instituted various quota systems on foreign media imports. While Canada, because it borders the United States, is somewhat special, Toronto can still be used as an example to dramatize the growing impact of U.S. media on other countries. If the six Toronto television stations used no more than 40 percent of U.S. programs (as directed by the Canadian CRTC* guidelines), they would still show 336 hours of U.S. TV products a week, or 17,472 hours a year.

While television is getting the lion's share of the attention, the U.S. print media are also very active in ways that will increase cultural impact abroad. Computers, video display printers which can plug into telephone or telex systems, and electronic satellite transmission are transforming the way U.S. newspapers and magazines are written, mocked up, and printed. *The Wall Street Journal, Time,* and others have been using long-distance printing domestically for some time, and the *New York Times* is using this technique to bring out a Chicago edition. But in spring 1980, *Time* magazine began to transmit its entire magazine to Hong Kong by satellite.

---

* Canadian Radio-television and Telecommunications Commission.

Printed there, the international edition goes on sale before the U.S. edition hits the street. *The Wall Street Journal* is following the same process for printing in Hong Kong, and the Paris-based *International Herald Tribune* has announced that it will do the same, with same-day delivery throughout Asia.[8]

Media Diplomacy

With changing technologies, new opportunities for using the media for political purposes are arising. Consider the following examples.

President Carter steps off the plane in Riyadh, Saudi Arabia, and burnoosed Saudi cameramen race up, portable video cameras on their shoulders. And—surprise! surprise!—the late afternoon Saudi arrival of the American president just happens to coincide with the airing time of the early morning U.S. TV network shows, *Good Morning, America* and *Today*. The material, sent by satellite to the networks in real time, is instantly viewed all over the United States. Arrivals of important personages anywhere in the world are now routinely scheduled by their staffs to meet the domestic political needs of the visiting leader. This sort of thing has long been done, but it is again a question of magnitude and instant impact.

The Pope takes an African trip and visits Zaire, Kenya, Ghana, Upper Volta, and the Ivory Coast. Each country has a satellite ground station, so that every day, television material can be transmitted directly to stations worldwide.

This type of instant coverage was impossible before 1976, when the portable video camera—the "minicam"—came into use. The minicam records both picture and sound on a tape cassette for instant use just like sound on a tape recorder. By eliminating cumbersome cables, thousands of pounds of equipment, and the time-consuming and tedious need to process film, television crews can work almost anywhere. Editing can be accomplished on a portable machine wherever electricity is available.

The advent of communications satellites has been even more important. The portable video camera, which needs only one cable to a truck with a microwave hookup, sends the picture to a television station nearby. (Or the cassette, edited or not, can just be taken there.) The television station then sends the picture up to a communications satellite, 22,300 miles away in geostationary orbit. The satellite sends the picture back down to another ground receiving station, which may be hundreds or thousands of miles from the first. The receiving station sends the picture by microwave or land line to a television station. The television station puts it on the air for the local audience.

A long-drawn-out, cumbersome procedure? Not at all! The whole process takes just seconds. And when DBS-TV becomes a reality, several of these middlemen will have been eliminated. Says an article in *Foreign Policy:*[9]

The first convergence of the jet-age correspondent, satellite transmission, portable video tape, and a government skillful at promoting its image abroad came in Egypt in 1977. The Sadat mission has often been characterized as "media diplomacy."

Sadat's use of the media (and Walter Cronkite) to expedite a diplomatic process caused a lot of raised eyebrows and dropped jaws. But it was, in general, considered constructive. The destructive side of the coin flipped up with Khomeini, who brought the use of the media for diplomacy by terrorism to full flower in one fell swoop.

Satellite transmission now available to newsmen makes the coverage of the Vietnam War—considered so *avant garde* then—seem a primitive affair, says the same article:

However, the technology that has made this kind of coverage possible has been accompanied by a growing sophistication on the part of governments, especially those in the Third World, and of revolutionary groups. They have learned how to use technology to manipulate the news.

The terrorists in the U.S. embassy in Tehran from November 1979 to April 1980 had their own television cameras and their own microwave system linked to VVIR (Iranian TV). And the world breathlessly awaited their special news events. On April 8, 1980, the three U.S. networks obtained an "Easter" videotape of the hostages produced by the terrorists. With three hours' notice to bring hostage families to local television stations (for previewing and comment on the film before parts were shown on TV) the networks jointly handled the videotape this way:[10]

- Iranian television sent the picture by satellite to London for conversion from a non-American to an American signal.
- London sent the picture back to a satellite.
- The satellite sent the picture to New York and the networks.
- The networks sent it back to a satellite and out to the local stations. A couple of local stations had to get the last leg by land line.

But from Tehran to Bellevue, Nebraska; Columbia, South Carolina; Chicago; and the U.S. West Coast, it was all accomplished in seconds.

We all watched the hostages come home stage by stage in real time, and television so dominated U.S. lives during the ensuing few days that Eric Sevareid, in a guest spot on CBS evening news, was prompted to comment:[11] "TV has been the national hearth, the ingathering, the place of prayer."

U.S. television stations, unlike those even in most Western democracies, are not government owned. While the United States does restrict foreign ownership of television and radio stations, the U.S. stations have programming freedom. Despite this, according to UNESCO figures,[12] the United States has the dubious distinction of ranking next to the People's Republic of China as the lowest on the list of the world's countries in importing foreign television programs. This is mainly a commercial question, but in some ways it makes the United States, the world's richest nation in communications and information resources, one of the world's most culturally deprived nations in terms of access not only to foreign television programming, but also to foreign books, newspapers, magazines, films, and news.

This isolation makes it hard for the United States to understand the reactions of other nations to the constant U.S. media presence. But, as military means for solving modern international problems become less and less desirable, the understanding of men's minds takes on more and more importance. At the end of World War II, large numbers of nations were basically sympathetic to and attracted by American ideals and ideas. But this is not altogether true any more. That it is not true may be due in no small part to this one-way media street.

The new media technologies, especially the portable video camera and satellite broadcast transmission, offer a great deal of hope for remedying this situation. Ten years ago, less than half of all television news stories in the United States were shown on the day they happened. Now, ordinarily only special features or light closing stories are more than one day old. And ten years ago, it cost $4000 to get a line to send television material from Seattle to New York. Today, by satellite, it costs $400. Costs from the Far East and Middle East to New York have been halved in the meantime and those from Europe reduced even more sharply. The portable video camera, videotape, satellite transmission, and falling costs have meant that the number of foreign news stories covered by NBC TV rose from 334 in 1976 to 806 in 1979, and those by ABC TV rose from 530 in 1977 to 900 in 1979.[13]

SPECIFIC INTERNATIONAL PROBLEM AREAS

Part II

"Free Flow Forever" vs. "Objective and Balanced News"

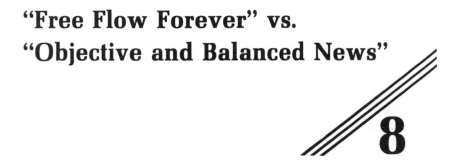

8

The imbalances which are a feature of communication flows the world over represent serious obstacles to Third World countries in their efforts to achieve positive development, as well as hindering attempts to promote genuine co-operation, on an equal footing, between them and the industrialized countries.

Until now, certain regions and certain categories of people spoke and the rest listened. This situation can no longer be tolerated. . . .[1]

THERE are many contradictions from country to country in the demands of the various developing nations regarding communications and information. But there is clearly an enormous distance between U.S. insistence on the sanctity of the free flow of international news regardless of any other consideration, and the collective developing world demand that news about their countries be reported on their terms. The U.S. position in this conflict has been referred to by critics as insistence on "free flow forever," and the developing world calls its position a demand for "objective and balanced" reporting of the news.

There are three related parts to this North-South confrontation, which has been playing itself out through the United Nations. The first is a demand by the developing nations for a New International Economic Order, which only marginally concerns communication and information problems. But closely related to this is a second demand for a New International Information Order. This involves information in its broadest sense and deals with the various economically oriented types of information such as data processing, as well as with the more traditional types of media and cultural matters. Parallel with these broad information concerns, the developing nations then made a third demand, for a mass media resolution to deal specifically with international news and news gatherers.

Third World Demands

The demand for a New International Economic Order, which grew up during the 1960s and 1970s, has to do with the insistence of the developing countries on a redistribution of the world's wealth. This involves a new division of labor, and new rules for international trade and monetary affairs— with more advantage tilted toward themselves. The United States initially considered this preposterous, especially in its first bald presentation. But, by 1977, the U.S. Representative to the United Nations, Ambassador Young, was able to say that the underlying objectives were ones which could be agreed upon, although nations could argue forever on the means for attaining them.

The closely related proposed New International Information Order is based on a number of principles which the United States and other developed nations generally consider laudable, such as:[2]

• Communication is a key factor of cultural independence, which itself is inseparable from political independence.

- The growing gulf dividing those countries able freely to disseminate their messages from those which do not have this possibility raises problems which affect the whole world and have pernicious consequences for both developing and developed countries.
- The interdependence between developed and developing countries is increasing in this area, as in others, a factor which justifies and should facilitate assistance to countries wishing to strengthen their communications capacities.
- All population sectors within each country and all countries, regardless of their development level, should have opportunities for making known their problems, their situations, and their aspirations.
- One-way communications should give way to the all-around exchanges of messages, and vertical communications should be supplemented by horizontal communications.
- The exchange of ideas, news, messages, and cultural works should help to reduce existing imbalances without prejudice to the sovereignty and dignity of all peoples or their cultural identity.
- A constant enlargement of the information flow should be sought through closer and more equitable collaboration in cultural activities and in the exchange of ideas and information.

But when attempts were made to put these lofty words into practice, they immediately became mired down in contradictory meanings. Among other things, no agreement could be reached on the definition of "news" or on what the proper function of the media might be.

News was generally defined by the developed countries as:[3] "A statement or report of an event which commands the attention of society." But extreme totalitarian countries went so far as to say that news was:[4] "Any statement or reported event which can be used to advance state objectives."

The American press has defined the function of the media as being that of a messenger; a bearer of tidings, whether good or bad. But other nations are said to see the press as a political agent, even if it is used for such things as:[5] ". . . strengthening peace and understanding, promoting human rights, and countering racism, apartheid, and incitement to war."

Various countries could thus employ the media for various honorable or dishonorable purposes.

Only 22 of the world's more than 150 nations can really be said to share U.S. views on freedom of the press. And even these, including most Western democracies, feel a need to apply some brakes. Within the United States itself, the domestic interpretation of First Amendment rights of the press—and especially of the electronic media—is constantly changing. This is indicated by numerous relatively recent Supreme Court decisions.[6] The view being advocated by the United States internationally is therefore considerably less flexible than that in use at home.

Despite some differences, there is still a general agreement in the developed world on the necessity for a press free to gather and disseminate international news. This is in exact opposition to the view of some developing country spokesmen, who assert that they must control news reports so that: "The truth will be made available to the rest of the world."

Translating this sort of wording into action, Tanzania and Nigeria have adopted laws which give their national news agencies exclusive rights to gather and disseminate all domestic news both for domestic and for international purposes. Many other developing countries have instituted practices of restricting news coverage to official sources, restricting access to news, denying visas to reporters, and physical and mental harassment and even imprisonment of news gatherers.*

The Soviet Union and other communist countries are, of course, the classic offenders in the area of free flow of news. In 1975, however, at the Conference on Security and Cooperation in Europe—the so-called Helsinki conference—35 nations, including communist ones, proclaimed:[8] ". . . the right of journalists to gather news without restraint." This declaration has had little practical effect on official communist country

---

* Specific states which have been cited for abuse or restriction of journalists are: Algeria, Argentina, Central African Empire, Chile, Cuba, Czechoslovakia, Ethiopia, German Democratic Republic, Haiti, Israel, Laos, Lebanon, Libya, Mozambique, Nicaragua, Nigeria, Pakistan, Paraguay, Peru, Poland, People's Republic of China, Philippines, Somalia, Syria, Tanzania, Uruguay, USSR, Yugoslavia, and Zaire.[7]

behavior toward either its own domestic or foreign reporters. It is nevertheless significant that democratic and communist states could agree, at least in principle, on such a statement, since this gives moral support for future improvement in this area.

It is important to note that events leading up to the preparations for the UNESCO Mass Media Resolution which was adopted in the fall of 1978 were not primarily instigated by the Soviet Union, notwithstanding its active participation. The USSR is usually willing to fish in troubled waters and to help U.S. diplomats earn their keep, and this project had great ideological appeal for the Soviets. But the Mass Media Resolution was the result of developing world discontent, and it would be a mistake not to recognize that.

It should also be pointed out that developing countries are of many different kinds and are often seeking very different ends. Each developing nation has many and often contradictory needs, as does the United States and every other country in the world. Developing countries range from those governed by the most malignant types of dictatorships with no pretense to a free press to those closely akin to the philosophical positions of the Western democracies. Some developing nations have very old and entrenched cultures while others are seeking a sense of identity for the first time. Some have an established upper class which likes its own privileged position and wishes little or nothing to do with the masses of the country's population. Others have newly educated—often U.S.- or Western-educated—elite groups who may want to help their fellow countrymen but feel estranged from them. In some countries the requirements of religion contradict the desire for modernization. In others the perceived need to conceal inadequacies may outweigh the country's desire to have its story told. Some developing nations are poor and some—the oil-producing countries—are rich. Some have plentiful native resources to exploit while others have few or almost none.

The conflicting needs of the ruling elites themselves account for many contradictions. These people, especially those who have been Western educated, may want to—even demand to—read *Time* and *Newsweek,* etc., and watch American films and television shows. They may insist upon access to AP and UPI tickers. But at the same time they feel guilty and confused, for they know how dependent they and their countries are on foreign information sources. It makes them realize, too, just how far they have personally grown away from their own "native" cultures. And, in some instances, they do not want the general population disturbed by the vision of modern technologies, which they, the leaders, are unable to provide.

All these conflicting needs were present when the delegates from 146 nations met at the 20th General Assembly of UNESCO in Paris to draft a Mass Media Resolution on how international news should be handled in the future. The basic document on which the Resolution was to be based was the Report of the International Commission for the Study of Communication Problems (the MacBride Commission).[9] This Commission had been studying the problem since 1976.

The Commission study was an attempt by UNESCO to deal politically with the perception of virtually all the developing countries that most media flow and flow of cultural commodities is directed *into* their countries *from* the developed world and that almost none of the flow is the other way. The developing countries complain that they are being inundated with Western—primarily American—media and information products, with no reciprocal flow from them. At the same time, they charge, Western journalists report only bad things about them—news of crimes, violence, disasters, riots, and so on. They say that Western journalists don't "say what we want said," and that, even when satisfactory types of news are reported, this news is presented to the world from the point of view of the West. A Sri Lanka diplomat to the United Nations is said to have objected to having his people characterized as "breeding like rabbits" when, he said, you could make the same point by saying that they are "no longer dying like flies." The Western press was also accused of making a fuss over the relatively small number of whites killed in the 1978 war in Zaire while virtually ignoring the much higher number of deaths among blacks.

Among the charges, it is said that the five major wire services, and especially the uninhibited western services, Associated Press, United Press International, Agence France Presse, and Reuters,* give only developed-country views. The developing countries have therefore demanded that these wire service "monopolies" be broken up and replaced by "more balanced news gathering agencies."

The Mass Media under Fire

Until protests arose from the developing nations, the principle embodied in Article 19 of the Universal Declaration of Human Rights: "Everyone has the right to freedom of opinion and expression; this right includes freedom to hold opinions . . . and to seek, receive and impart information and ideas through any media and regardless of frontiers" had formed the basis of a common understanding on the free flow of news among nations outside the communist bloc. This remains the cornerstone of U.S. foreign policy on information. This 1948 United Nations General Assembly declaration was a key post-World War II document, and a clear effort to prevent future excesses by totalitarian governments of the sort which the war had just been fought to eliminate. However, this declaration was made when only about one-third of the world's present nations existed and when developing countries were either still colonial possessions or otherwise had little influence. It is therefore not surprising that the legitimacy of this precept, which they took little part in formulating, would be called into question by the developing world.

These protests were also in response to the steadily increasing technical capability of the developed countries to prepare and distribute greater and greater quantities of information products.

---

* The fifth is the Soviet Union's Tass.

The first resolution drafted at this 1978 UNESCO meeting included passages incompatible with the traditions and interests of the United States and other developed countries. It imposed obligations on members of the press and restrictions on their behavior, and gave rights—even obligations—to individual governments to determine and enforce the "proper" behavior of news gatherers and publishing industries. While UNESCO resolutions have no effect of law, it was felt by the advocates of free news flow that such inclusions in a resolution by this prestigious organization would lend great support to governments bent on imposing restrictions.

An acceptable compromise resolution was then negotiated, which maintained some of the concepts of "objective and balanced" news, but removed the rights and obligations of states to oversee the press. The compromise also referred to Article 19 of the Universal Declaration of Human Rights, and included a positive statement concerning free flow of information to balance every negative statement permitted to stand.

The end result was pronounced to be a triumph by the U.S. policymakers. But the U.S. media went up in smoke. The *New York Times* ran an editorial saying:[10]

Western diplomats are congratulating themselves on having turned a dangerous international declaration on the obligations of the press into an incomprehensible hodge-podge of slogans and prescriptions. The great "compromise" declaration of the United Nations Educational Scientific and Cultural Organization (UNESCO) now stands adopted, a triumph of obfuscation. If it is no longer a clear and present threat to news agencies, it remains in language and spirit an affront to the very idea of communication. The world deserves to know that the Americans who accepted it as the least offensive document they could write with 145 other nations were not speaking for the free press of the United States.

This was, of course, meant to reiterate the most orthodox interpretation of the First Amendment rights of the U.S. press. But it is true that, in making the compromise, the United

States, for the first time, accepted the notion that content is negotiable and a subject suitable for government discussion. Up until this Resolution, the United States had steadfastly contended that this was not the case.

The Resolution, however, did not end the argument. No sooner had the ink dried on this compromise than the MacBride Commission set about to deal with every item which had not been agreed upon. The problem was also taken to the United Nations General Assembly a few days after the UNESCO conference and the subject picked up there from scratch. So far, very little action has been taken, however.

During 1979 and 1980, the MacBride Commission developed a "final report"[11] for presentation at the Fall 1980 UNESCO General Assembly meeting in Belgrade. This report quite strongly endorsed the right of the press to report the news, and even insisted on the right of the press to interview any news source, including dissidents and opposition party members. It endorsed, in fact, much of the developed country view, but it did recommend breaking up the five major news "cartels."

While the United States has expressed shock over developing country accusations against the wire services, it should be noted that, in the 1920s and 1930s, the Associated Press, then a struggling little organization engaged in combat with the giant Reuters, voiced complaints against that organization very similar to those being heard from the developing countries today.[12] The General Manager of the Associated Press, Kent Cooper, accused Reuters at that time of: ". . . a domination the likes of which, for international ramifications, complications, and regimentation of the world opinion has never been equalled . . ." and said that Reuters decided what news would come out of America: "It told the world about Indians on the warpath in the West, lynchings in the South, and bizarre crimes in the North."

Cooper said that according to Reuters: "It wasn't safe to travel (in the U.S.) on account of the Indians." He also said that Reuters served the economic interests of England in world trade, and constantly stressed England's superior culture.

Domestically, Americans are quick to point out that crime, violence, and disasters are all they ever hear from their own press and television, and that "very little good news is ever reported." States like Kansas complain that they are only heard from nationally when they have a tornado or a blizzard. And that even the tornado or blizzard is seen through Eastern eyes.

The news media say that their better technologies will gradually permit them to bring outlying areas into the mainstream as more and more coverage becomes possible. This will most probably extend into the international area (it already does to a point) and could alleviate a part of this problem. On the other hand, increased activity, especially in a hostile political climate, could simply increase aggravation.

There is no doubt that the developing nations do have very valid grievances. News and cultural information flow *is* basically one-way. But developing nations, like other nations, want high-quality information products for the lowest price, and are buying them from the cheapest source, the United States.

Competing Values

Some developing nations have begun to limit the number of Western-produced films and television programs which can be shown in their countries. In this way they have taken their cue from Canada, the United Kingdom, and Australia, which are also setting limits. A news exchange service called the Nonaligned News Pool has also been created as one attempt to get more balanced news coverage. So far it is mainly confined to reporting government press releases for lack of other material. This will probably change with the better training of reporters.

Most developing nations are trying to establish their own news sources as a supplement to Western news agencies and Tass. But several developing countries are demanding restric-

DISTRIBUTION OF FOREIGN AND DOMESTIC
NEWS BY SOME LARGE U.S. NEWSPAPERS

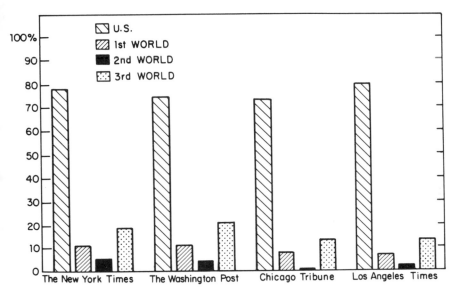

Despite allegations to the contrary, key U.S. newspapers give more extensive coverage to Third World events than they do to other foreign news. (Based on Edward T. Pinch, "A Brief Study on News Patterns in Sixteen Third World Countries," *Murrow Reports,* The Fletcher School of Law and Diplomacy, Tufts University, April 1978. Reprinted by permission.)

tions on reporters entering their countries, the right of their government to control foreign reporters, and the right to reply to stories they feel are biased or simply unpleasant.

All of this makes for a lot of hard feeling in many areas between the developing and the developed world which might not be necessary if the attitudes adopted at both extremes could be more flexible.

Former Director of the U.S. International Communications Agency Ambassador Reinhardt suggested that the right to free flow of information, either within the United States domestically or in the international arena, is not absolute. He said that the free flow of information should be considered a "preferred freedom" with "presumptive validity" which "must bend to admit other values only if there is no other way to realize the competing value." But, he has said:[13] ". . . there are competing values, such as personal privacy, cultural integrity, national sovereignty, and distributive justice . . ." which are of great social importance and must also be given maximum scope.

To implement such subtle suggestions as these calls for great sophistication and fine tuning of policy response. The United States is still neither institutionally nor psychologically prepared for such implementation.

While the establishment of two-way news flow is vital, much more is involved here than a threat to "First Amendment rights." The New World Information Order should be recognized as an increasingly coherent attempt to shift a portion of world power from the advanced to the developing countries. It therefore embodies the most basic issues now dividing the North and South.

Whether the United States and other developed nations like it or not, it seems clear that some form of New International Information Order *will* evolve over the next few years. The question to be faced by the advanced countries is how to marshal the forces essentially in favor of free flow of news to find solutions satisfactory to all sides. This could prevent radicalization and domination of the situation by those basically hostile to the very concept of free information flow.

Transborder Data Flow (TBDF)* Restrictions

9

WITH the first subconscious recognition that something new, important, and disturbing was happening all across the communications and information spectrum internationally, government and business leaders—primarily in advanced countries—began to clutch onto TBDF as a somewhat discrete thing which they could attempt to control. The very term "transborder data flow" thus became a kind of shorthand through which nations could express their fears about a changing future and could plot possible ways to "do something" about it.

By defining transborder data flow as "the flow across borders of any kind of material which is computer readable,"† it seemed for a time that this one problem might indeed be circumscribed and held within manageable bounds. But the problem is much wider than at first supposed. The following

---

* TDF is another abbreviation in use, but it ignores the all-important border.

† Most European national data protection laws and the Council of Europe draft treaty on privacy deal only with computer readable data.

THE ENVIRONMENT OF TRANSBORDER DATA FLOW

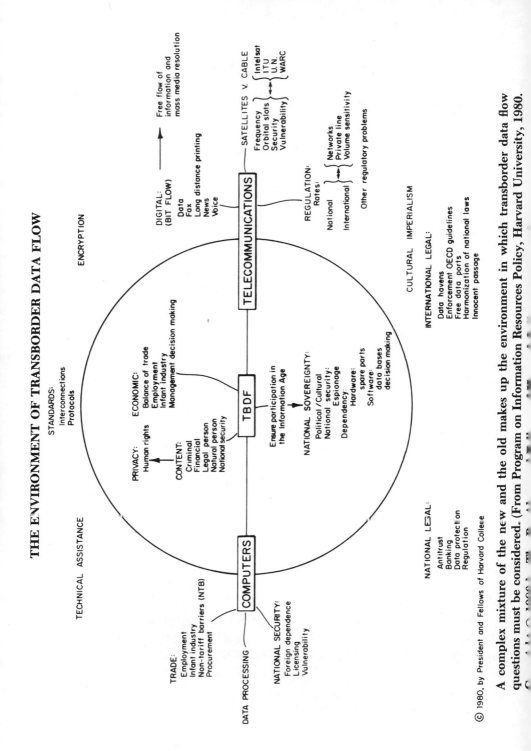

STANDARDS:
Interconnections
Protocols

ENCRYPTION

TECHNICAL ASSISTANCE

DIGITAL:
(BIT FLOW)
Data
Fax
Long distance printing
News
Voice

→ Free flow of information and mass media resolution

SATELLITES V. CABLE
Frequency
Orbital slots { Intelsat ITU U.N. WARC }
Security
Vulnerability

REGULATION:
Rates:
National
International { Networks Private line Volume sensitivity }

Other regulatory problems

TELECOMMUNICATIONS

PRIVACY:
Human rights

CONTENT:
Criminal
Financial
Legal person
Natural person
National security

ECONOMIC:
Balance of trade
Employment
Infant industry
Management decision making

TBDF

Ensure participation in the Information Age

NATIONAL SOVEREIGNTY:
Political/Cultural
National security:
Espionage
Dependency:
Hardware:
spare parts
Software:
data bases
decision making

CULTURAL IMPERIALISM

INTERNATIONAL LEGAL:
Data havens
Enforcement OECD guidelines
Free data ports
Harmonization of national laws
Innocent passage

COMPUTERS

DATA PROCESSING

TRADE:
Employment
Infant industry
Non-tariff barriers (NTB)
Procurement

NATIONAL SECURITY:
Foreign dependence
Licensing
Vulnerability

NATIONAL LEGAL:
Antitrust
Banking
Data protection
Regulation

© 1980, by President and Fellows of Harvard College

A complex mixture of the new and the old makes up the environment in which transborder data flow questions must be considered. (From Program on Information Resources Policy, Harvard University, 1980.

chart, with TBDF at the center, shows the complex mixture of the new and the old which makes up the environment in which transborder data flow questions must be considered. Every transborder activity of government, business, military, or financial import is affected, including the all-important world currency market.

Electronic Border Breach

Computer readable transborder data flow began in the 1950s with airline reservations and with defense command and control networks. It increased steadily during the 1960s, through the activities of multinational corporations, financial, educational, and religious institutions, labor unions, and so on. But, in the 1970s, with increases in computer effectiveness, satellite activities, and the digitization of information, TBDF began to pose changes of a magnitude really disturbing to a variety of nations. Many of the worries of these nations focused on data banks and bases and centered around the activities of the fast-growing data processing industry.

As the flow of information across borders burgeoned, the need for data banks in centralized places which could be accessed from multiple locations sprang up. The market for data bases increased at a formidable rate as well, growing from 10,000 customers in 1965 to two million in 1978. By that year, there were 362 data banks, 208 of which were located in the United States. Eighty percent of all data bases for these banks worldwide still consists of U.S.-originated data.[1]

The customers for these data bases came to include not only national and multinational corporations of all types, and the financial, educational, and other institutions of many countries, but also quasi-governmental organizations and governments themselves. Two classic examples which are often cited are those of the Swedish fire department, whose equipment is activated by a General Electric data bank in Cleveland, Ohio, and the French Five-Year Plan, which is stored in a U.S. data bank. Another frequently cited case is that of some Eastern European airline reservation systems which are handled from computers in Georgia (U.S.).

As it became more and more commonplace for data originating in one country to be processed and stored in another, three major international issues concerning transborder data flow began to emerge. The first and most vocal of these issues is concerned with the possibility of the violation of the privacy of individual persons. Originating in Sweden, this concern was quickly embraced by other developed nations such as France and Germany. The second issue, which has tended to be downplayed, is a matter of raw money. Who will reap the profits of this information business, which is already enormous and has as yet unknown potential? The third issue deals with the somewhat more elusive but perhaps politically more important concepts of national pride, national sovereignty, and national insecurity.

Nations are also concerned that critical records which could be needed for internal governmental actions, or data related to domestic economic growth are stored outside their country and therefore outside their control. In some instances, it is felt that national security is actually being threatened. But more often the concept of national sovereignty is involved. There is a vague sense that it is "not right" or is a national shame for one nation to be dependent on another for data or for data processing and storage of materials which could be critical to domestic industrial or governmental tasks. In addition, some countries are saying that the United States imports raw data and exports finished information, while most other countries export raw data and import finished information. This transfer of the description of the "colony to mother country" relationship from classic economics to the information world perhaps does not make sense. The United States has, in any case, become an exporter of raw materials and an importer of finished goods in many manufacturing areas, becoming a "colony" also by this description.

These combined fears about transborder data flow have led to attempts at national control by a wide variety of countries.

United States corporations, which have the most sophisticated data bank equipment and bases, and the most flexible and least expensive data processing and storage services, have attracted the major share of the world's customers. They are, therefore, the main targets of the proposed restrictions.

Privacy Needs

Much has happened to blur the concept of privacy in the West since the English statesman William Pitt the Elder said in the eighteenth century:[2]

The poorest man may in his cottage bid defiance to all the force of the Crown. It may be frail: its roof may shake; the wind may blow through it; the storms may enter, the rain may enter—but the King of England cannot enter; all his forces dare not cross the threshold of the ruined tenement.

But privacy is still considered a basic human right and, indeed, a basic tenet of civilization.

That Americans are concerned with privacy domestically was made very clear by a Harris poll in 1979,[3] which showed that by nearly two to one, Americans have a sense of real concern about personal privacy threats. As Senator Mathias has put it:[4]

The (American) Founding Fathers could not foresee the electronic age. They could not foresee telephones, wiretaps, bugging devices, computers, and data banks. Technology has cluttered the domain of the Constitution. It has confused things. It has made our homes and our private lives accessible, even when our doors are locked and our shades are drawn. . . .

Other countries have similar but often more concrete privacy worries. The Western Europeans, recalling the havoc the Gestapo wrought with manila folders, are horrified at the persecution that could be perpetrated with the aid of computers.

In response to such concerns, government-sponsored privacy protection laws appeared in the United States and in all other advanced countries during the 1970s. Sweden has had a privacy law since 1973. Germany's law took effect at the beginning of 1978. The French Act on Information and Liberty was approved in the early part of that same year. Part IV of the Human Rights Bill of Canada on protection of personal information went into effect in 1977. Other laws or reports or inquiries regarding privacy were prepared in Austria, Belgium, Denmark, Luxembourg, the Netherlands, Norway, Spain, Australia, Ireland, Italy, Japan, Switzerland, and the United Kingdom during the 1970s.[5]

In the United States, the Privacy Act dates to 1974, but privacy protection has long been provided by the First and Sixth Amendments to the Constitution. The Fair Credit Reporting Act, which gives protection to the consumer, was also passed in 1971, and by 1978, some 300 privacy protection bills were pending in state legislatures and almost 100 bills had been drafted in the U.S. Congress.

Privacy as Trade Protective Device

United States privacy protection differs in four important respects from that of most other countries:

- The U.S. Privacy Act applies only to federal agencies, with some provisions for extension.
- As this privacy protection is extended, it will be applied only to particular segments of private enterprise on a selective basis.
- No U.S. privacy measure provides the statutory assurance that data sent into the United States will enjoy the same protection it does in its country of origin.
- The U.S. Privacy Act does not apply to foreign nationals or even to permanent resident aliens. However, most state and local legislation does not distinguish between U.S. citizens and foreign nationals.

European privacy laws are generally omnibus, applying to all persons engaged in data processing. A very basic difference in approach between the United States and the European countries is that, while the European legal tradition prefers the use of central administrative bodies to provide relief to individuals who feel themselves wronged, the American legal tradition is decentralized and provides for relief through the courts.

The various national laws on privacy, including those of the United States, are remarkably uniform regarding the principles of protection. They usually provide that the subject of the data must know about records kept on him, and that he must have access to the files and opportunities to correct errors. They also stipulate that the data must be relevant to the file, that access to the data be limited, and that legal remedies for misuse be given.

This uniformity of opinion is reflected in the OECD Voluntary Guidelines* which were developed in the late 1970s and were adopted in September 1980 by OECD member countries.[6] The Guidelines seek agreement between the governments of the OECD nations to accept certain common standards for privacy protection to which they will encourage their industries to adhere. The Guidelines are an attempt to arrive at some method of harmonization of the various national laws in order to achieve a common denominator for TBDF activities.

While the United States was second only to Sweden in enacting privacy legislation, Europeans say that the United States does not give sufficient attention to the question of privacy and does not understand that civil liberties are at stake. This criticism is unwarranted but is nevertheless creating a great deal of irritation in U.S.–Western European private and official circles. A major problem involved in the whole privacy debate is that Americans, especially American businessmen, but also some government officials, are skeptical of the supposedly al-

* The Organization for Economic Cooperation and Development is composed of the following members: Australia, Austria, Belgium, Canada, Denmark, Federal Republic of Germany, Finland, France, Greece, Iceland, Ireland, Italy, Japan, Luxembourg, Netherlands, New Zealand, Norway, Portugal, Spain, Sweden, Turkey, United Kingdom, United States of America, and Yugoslavia.

truistic reasons behind many of the national privacy measures. To be blunt, there is a strong belief that, while privacy is indeed a bona fide issue in itself, "privacy" is often a thin disguise for economic protectionism.

Governments and industries around the world are extremely concerned about the economic aspects of TBDF, which is daily becoming more profitable. Foreign nations claim that data leaving their countries for processing and storage elsewhere is a cause of balance of trade losses. It is certainly true that the U.S. data processing industries contribute positively to the U.S. balances of payments and trade. Other countries also claim that data processing outside their borders takes away jobs and deprives their own national workers of the chance to develop technical and managerial skills related to the industry. Above all, nations fear that the concentration of data processing facilities, management, and research and development in the United States lowers the chances of their own countries of moving into the forefront of a wide spectrum of the latest technological developments.

Canada has been exceptionally vocal about this, being very frank to admit that its concerns with transborder data flow are mainly economic and political. And Canada has acted on these worries by proposing legislation which would prohibit the flow, processing, or storage of certain types of data—banking and financial—outside the country.[7] Suggestions have even been made by the Canadian government that data processing related to Canadian business operations be required to be performed within the country unless otherwise specifically authorized. Since a high percentage of Canadian business is intertwined with American firms, this is aimed at making U.S. companies who operate in Canada leave their data processing there.

Great care must be taken not to lump together all computer readable data which flows across borders. Data on individuals, with the major exception of airlines reservations, is said, in fact, to be only a small portion of the total transmitted by companies. Manufacturing, engineering, construction, and consumer products industries are included in one study.[8] Most of the TBDF was found to be of a financial, technical, inventory, or other nonpersonal nature, and thus falls outside the concern for individual privacy. It has also been reported in Europe, that more than 50 percent of all transatlantic transborder communications is flow between corporate subdivisions. Interference with this kind of transborder data flow would be equivalent to cutting off interoffice mail.

The governments of developing countries, several of which are becoming active in data markets, are also taking restrictive steps. Venezuela has prohibited the export of all data for processing and storage. Mexico's national information policy contains a clause that data flows must be "in the national interest." Brazil claims that the United States is "dumping" time-sharing services in other countries, and thus requires specific approval of all international teleprocessing links, renewable every three years.

The Economic Squeeze Play

Meanwhile, the government-owned Post, Telephone, and Telegraph Administrations (PTTs) of Western Europe and Japan, which provide services, set prices, and also regulate various computer communications activities, have threatened less open but possibly more effective types of control. Several ways have been devised, with at least the threat of implementation, to cut down on the competitiveness of U.S. data processing companies. Among these are included higher tariffs for leased or private lines, denial of applications for new private circuits, revocation of existing private facilities with their replacement by public ones, and various kinds of national pressures.

Most PTTs have two basic functions: They must provide the whole range of communications services necessary for the support of their country's national needs and interests, and they must see to it that the telecommunications services earn enough money to subsidize the costly postal service.

During the period of rapid growth of the data communications activities in the 1960s and early 1970s, the various common carriers worldwide tended to keep their activities more or less confined to classical types of services. In the United States, this was due to regulatory restrictions, while in Europe and Japan, it was essentially an oversight. The result was that a wide variety of private communications service networks sprang up, using the transmission facilities of the regular telecommunications agencies but tailoring the hardware and software of private corporations to their special needs. These private service networks raced so far ahead with new technologies, and the common carriers lagged so far behind, that by 1980 the private service networks used by U.S. corporations abroad could provide services for one-eighth of the cost at which they could be obtained from the PTTs, when and if they could be obtained at all.

At first the PTTs welcomed the business of supplying the telecommunications facilities for these service networks because it was a great new source of income. But, as the private networks became capable of pushing greater and greater quantities of data through the telecommunications circuits at lower and lower cost, the PTTs began to see them as an economic threat both to themselves and to the data processing services of their country. It came to be recognized that the private lines were also cutting into the income from Telex and other profitable services provided by the PTTs. They were, in short, becoming dangerous rivals.

The PTTs have therefore belatedly put together various public networks, which they are "encouraging" U.S. corporations to use, although they cost much more and provide less service than can be had privately. The U.S. businesses see the primary aim of the PTTs at this time as being to penalize them for more efficient use of technology and to blunt their present competitive advantage.

So far, this has been mainly a battle of words. But it has created a sense of strain and uncertainty for all international business, and has caused a great deal of friction between U.S.

companies and foreign governments. Since the governments of most foreign countries are now also assuming active roles in furthering their own domestic data processing interests (by financing, loans, promotion of research and development, etc.), U.S. data communications and equipment industries are increasingly suggesting that the U.S. government should pay more attention to U.S. interests in this area. This is hardly a preposterous suggestion, since the data processing industry is one of the few U.S. industries now producing a large positive balance of trade. The broader problem is that these proposed restrictions would affect *any* U.S. business or industry operating internationally. While some congressional testimony to this end has been given by the Commerce and State Departments,[9] it remains to be seen whether this will be followed up by concrete action.

Organizing Internationally

Presently, the Council of Europe, the Organization for Economic Cooperation and Development (OECD), the European Community (EC), and the International Chamber of Commerce (ICC) are all attempting to deal with the transborder data flow questions of the industrialized nations. The Intergovernmental Bureau for Informatics (IBI), an offshoot of UNESCO, concerns itself, meanwhile, with the transborder data flow problems of the developing world. It is interesting to note that, notwithstanding a great deal of rhetoric to the contrary, the carefully worded policy statements of the developed-country-dominated ICC and the developing-country-dominated IBI are remarkably similar.

The ICC says:[10]

There is a need for international coherence of privacy-data protection legislation, and ICC should collaborate with appropriate national and international bodies to achieve this. . . .

At the same time, the ICC recognizes the variety of social and legal environments for which such legislation is framed. The ICC would prefer a flexible international framework which permits the widest possible collaboration between states which seek to protect the legitimate interests of their citizens. Wide collaboration is essential, both to provide a better guarantee of protection to the individual and to allow those responsible for the design and implementation of large scale data processing systems to cater for a near uniform set of legal requirements.

The IBI statement goes:[11]

The full benefits of data transmission as a tool for world development will depend on whether information resources are widely distributed and universally accessible; whether a decentralized decision-making process for matters affecting major national, regional, or worldwide interests will emerge; and whether the integrity and reliability of international communications is protected by a liberal legal regime, and not laid down from nationalistic or protectionist barriers which discourage open flows of data between countries.

There is therefore a wealth of interest extant in overcoming various barriers to transborder data flow even as such barriers are being erected. But great care is needed if nations are to cooperate and threats to transborder data flow are not to become more serious during the 1980s. A new proposition, called "vulnerability," is catching fire all across Europe. It says that all computer systems are terribly vulnerable to war, economic embargo, terrorism, error, and malfunction, and that any of these could lead to a "complete breakdown." Only 14 percent of all companies using computer systems, says a report by the Swedish Defense Ministry, could continue operations by manual power.[12] This proposition may be perfectly true, and the dangers of dependence on computers are only too real. But the proposed curative processes for this newly discovered malady would involve tightening up on data processing security requirements, insistence on local expertise for systems, limitations on the amount of foreign processing that can be done by multinationals, requirements for elaborate record keeping on exported data, "simplification" of computer systems, and other obstructive solutions familiar to those who have followed the history of the transborder data flow debate.

In the final analysis, other countries need the benefits engendered by transborder data flow at least as much as does the United States. And they are not losing as much on the deal as they would like the United States to believe. They can only restrict U.S. business activities so far without ending up by restricting themselves. But they can certainly create log jams, even if they are self-destructive ones. Many real problems on both sides, which are probably capable of resolution, are being obscured by rhetoric. These various problems need to be sought out and carefully examined. For without a more cooperative climate, everybody is going to lose. With a more cooperative climate, everybody can gain—a lot. The OECD Voluntary Guidelines on privacy of personal data are a good beginning. But they are just a beginning.

Dividing Up the Spectrum: WARC '79

10

AFTER four years of preparation involving more than half a dozen U.S. government agencies, the Congress, and the private sector, a U.S. delegation of 69 people set off for Geneva in September 1979. There they would join nearly 2000 delegates from 149 other countries for a ten-week twentieth-century marathon.

The occasion: The World Administrative Radio Conference (WARC '79).

The mandate: To consider some 15,000 proposals which would allocate world frequency bands until the next plenary conference—then scheduled for 1999.

The last such conference, which has been customarily held at twenty-year intervals, had taken place in 1959. But in the twenty-year time span since that plenary session of the International Telecommunication Union (ITU),* the geography

---

* ITU—International Telecommunication Union—is the organization responsible for the world's radio spectrum allocations. It is a specialized agency of the United Nations.

both of the world and of communications and information technology had radically changed. So, too, had the political, economic, social, and security stakes in communications and information of all nations involved.

In 1959, representatives of 86 nations—for the most part the like-minded industrialized states—had sat down at the conference table to discuss the spectrum's future. In 1979, the number of ITU members had grown from 96 to 154. Most of the new participants were from developing nations, and brought with them new points of view, priorities, aspirations, and—especially—fears.

In 1959, most satellites did not yet exist. The merger of computers and telecommunications technologies commercially was far in the future. Mobile radio for commercial and emergency purposes was still in its infancy. So were communications and information technologies like the various copying processes. Direct broadcasting via satellite for television was not even considered a practical possibility. Color television had just become commercially feasible. The telephone system was still "old-fashioned." And remote sensing from outer space was just a dream.

The high stakes involved in WARC were reflected in the intense emotion of many people regarding the issues, including members of the U.S. Congress and people high in the Administration. Dire predictions were made that the Conference would be politicized, and delegates would not stick to the technical and administrative agenda items. It was feared that extraneous political issues, such as Zionism or apartheid, might sidetrack the Conference, or that broader issues, such as the New World Information Order, or free flow of information, or freedom of the press, or prior consent for direct broadcasting television, might bog down more specific discussions.

And there was much reason for fear, since the Conference offered a distinct opportunity for a direct confrontation of the nastiest sort between the developed and the developing world.

The developing world saw a period ahead when, while it

THE RADIO SPECTRUM

BAND	FREQUENCIES	SOME USES
	From 300,000 to 3,000,000 MHz (or 300 to 3000 GHz)	Unallocated Spectrum
EHF (Extremely High Frequencies)	From 30,000 to 300,000 MHz (or 30 to 300 GHz)	Microwave relay for data transmission, radar, space research, short range military communications, experimental
SHF (Super High Frequencies)	From 3,000 to 30,000 MHz (or 3 to 30 GHz)	Communications satellites, microwave relay for phone messages, DBS-TV, deep space, space research, radar, air navigation, military communication, telemetry, radio-astronomy
UHF (Ultra High Frequencies)	From 300 to 3,000 MHz	Weather satellites, microwave relay for ovens and other equipment, UHF TV, radar, air navigation, space tracking, police, taxis, and ambulances
VHF (Very High Frequencies)	From 30 to 300 MHz	Military satellites, telemetry, VHF TV, FM radio, space tracking, air navigation and distress, police, taxis, and ambulances, world-wide radio-navigation
HF (High Frequencies)	From 3 to 30 MHz	Medium and long range communications, international broadcasting, shortwave radio, CB, air-ground, long range military communications

THE RADIO SPECTRUM

BAND	FREQUENCIES	SOME USES
MF (Medium Frequencies)	From .3 to 3 MHz (or 300 to 3000 kHz)	Medium and short range communications, air and marine navigation, AM radio, SOS, disaster, Ham radio, marine radiophone
LF (Low Frequencies)	From .03 to .3 MHz (or 30 to 300 kHz)	Long and medium range communications, air and marine navigation
VLF (Very Low Frequencies)	From .003 to .03 MHz (or 3 to 30 kHz)	Very long range military communications (+ 1000 nautical miles), time signals

Some of the activities taking place in the contested radio spectrum that the world must share. Over the past two decades, the geography both of the world and of communications and information technology has radically changed. (Adapted from U.S. State Department Special Report No. 57, August 1979.)

was still economically powerless, the advanced countries might divide up the radio frequencies of greatest commercial importance among themselves. Or at least they were seriously concerned with how the division might be done. Would the spectrum indeed be sliced in such a way that, when they needed more communications and could use more modern technologies, they would get a fair share? Or, would all the available frequencies be "used up" by then? They were very concerned that the existing system of "first come, first served"—in which a country can register a frequency with the ITU only when ready to make use of it—would leave no frequencies for their needs.

The United States and other Western countries had their own worries. The United States was concerned, first of all, with maintaining a very large portion of the spectrum for military and related uses. In this, it had the Soviet Union for an ally, since that country has very similar needs. The United

States was also interested in seeing satellite communications expanded, both for broadcasting and for data, facsimile, and other transmissions. The United States had before it a proposal of Satellite Business Systems (SBS) for a major program of data and teleconferencing communications via space. For this program to succeed, certain very high frequencies (VHF) must be available. The United States was also interested in expanding its domestic AM band to permit an additional 200 to 300 new radio stations to be owned by minorities. It was further interested in expanding the shortwave (HF) band for the use of transnational broadcasting, especially by the Voice of America and Radio Free Europe. This latter conflicted with the needs of developing countries, which still rely heavily on shortwave radio for general communications.

Every country attending had its own shopping list.

A major point of conflict between the developing and the developed countries centered around a priori assignment (or preassignment) of orbital positions and frequencies for space services, versus the "fair and equitable distribution" which was promised by the developed countries under the "first come, first served" system.

The developing countries felt that the spectrum should be planned—that is, divided up *now*, with certain frequencies allocated to members of the developing world whether or not those members could use them at present. A priori assignment was actually decided upon for certain uses of broadcasting satellites in some parts of the world in 1977. And in 1974, the frequency allotments for coast radiotelephone stations were preassigned.[1] In that instance, even landlocked countries with no use for frequencies of this nature were nevertheless assigned certain frequencies for this purpose. The United States and some other Western nations countered the arguments for advance assignment with the promise of "fair and equitable distribution" when the time came and assured the other nations that, through ever-advancing technology and other means, they would get their fair share whenever they were ready.

Another U.S. interest was in maintaining the integrity of the ITU, which in its view is the best mechanism for the orderly management of the frequencies. Some developing nations had expressed the opinion that this responsibility should be put under the more political framework of the United Nations General Assembly.[2]

Except for the first week, when there was a political confrontation over the election of a Chairman, the Conference went surprisingly well. Although the threat was ever-present, the feared North-South confrontations, bloc voting, and introduction of extraneous issues did not materialize. A large number of agenda items were successfully resolved. In general, U.S. industry and the U.S. delegation—which made about 900 proposals—were reasonably satisfied with the outcome. The U.S. telecommunications industry expressed the view that WARC had produced results:[3] ". . . that will allow American telecommunications companies to maintain existing operations while moving into innovative services. . . ."

The U.S. delegation officially said:[4]

We believe that WARC was successful in carrying out its objectives. While difficulties, both technical and political, were foreseen at the outset, we were impressed by the general absence of the latter and the ultimate satisfactory resolution of most of the former. Whatever concerns we may have about a few particular decisions taken by the conference, we believe that the conference Final Acts will provide a technical and regulatory framework for the expansion of communications facilities of the U.S. and abroad in the coming years, while maintaining a significant degree of order in allocating the spectrum among services.

United States proposals for allocation in the very high frequencies (above 40 GHz) were substantially adopted, and remote sensing, space research, and radio astronomy generally fared well. The conference remained on a technical plane, as the United States had hoped it would. The integrity of the ITU was preserved and the organization may actually have been strengthened.[5]

But most of the difficult issues were simply postponed. Space services in geostationary orbit, feeder links for the broadcasting satellite services, problems of high frequency band broadcasting services, and those of mobile services will all be subjects of a large series of planning conferences over the years to come. Thus, North-South confrontations on these subjects may have been merely delayed.

But this delay could not have been achieved had there been no communality of views and values. The desirability of attempting to resolve these types of issues through orderly international political processes and legitimate institutions was made evident and indicates a growing maturity on the part of all concerned. This augurs very well for the future.

By the end of the Conference, the "first come, first served" concept no longer remained unquestioned. And the number of reservations and footnotes entered would seem to be symptomatic of the highly increased technical complexity of communications and information and of its growing economic and political stakes. The State Department denies, however, that this has any particular significance.[6] The United States entered five reservations or formal statements that it would not be bound by particular Conference decisions. In the entire 115-year history of the ITU and its predecessor organizations, the United States had entered only one reservation before (in 1974).

Because of the postponements, there is much discussion about whether the Conference was not, in fact, a "failure." But dividing up the spectrum for the next twenty years in the face of vast and accelerating changes in communications and information was a losing proposition from the start. By yielding to the reality of today's world, nations may have, de facto, found a rational mechanism for dealing with these questions. If this indeed turns out to be the case, then an evolutionary step in international decision making has occurred which is far more important than any actual decisions taken or not taken at WARC '79.

Expanding International Satellite Capabilities and Two Controversial Activities

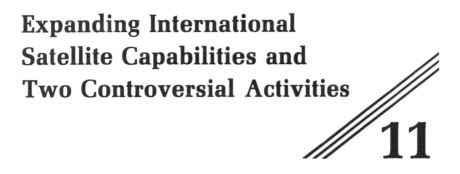

11

FOR almost two decades—the 1960s and most of the 1970s—the United States and the USSR held a monopoly on the world's satellite capabilities. Until recently, they were the only two countries with the combination of a large economic base, a large background industry and administrative management capability, and sufficient motivation to devote huge resources to the activity. They therefore maintained command of both launch capabilities and of the satellite technology itself.

But this situation is changing. France and Germany together now have an experimental communications satellite, the Symphonie. More important is the French Telecom I planned for 1984. This system, now an EC-wide effort, was designed as an answer to Satellite Business Systems and aimed at the business market.[1] And through French efforts especially, the European Space Agency (ESA) has a viable launch system called Ariane. Since the U.S. space shuttle, counted on for commercial use in the early 1980s, was seriously delayed, the Europeans are in a position to give the United States some real competition. Many entities outside ESA, including some in the United States, have already made down payments with Ariane for launches. INTELSAT, among others, has reserved three Ariane launches.

The most advanced experimental *communications* satellite in orbit to date is Canadian, but this was a joint U.S.–Canadian venture, launched by the National Aeronautics and Space Administration (NASA), with U.S. firms as prime contractors. The Japanese have the most advanced *broadcast* satellite in place, but it was made in America by GE–Valley Forge, launched by NASA, and turned over, in space, to Japan. The Japanese are using this experimental "bird" to broadcast television directly from the satellite into individual dish antennas.

The Japanese have also launched their own experimental communications satellite. China has a launch capability for other than commercial satellites. The United Kingdom has conducted a satellite launch. And in July 1980, India became the seventh country to join the satellite launch club. It is therefore just a matter of time before other nations become self-sufficient or competitive in the satellite area in general. This will increase the demands for radio frequency allocations and will undoubtedly bring about a "housing shortage" in outer space, where orbital slots are not unlimited. This may be ameliorated by technological advances. Frequency crowding is already being prepared for by some satellite systems, which are moving out to higher frequencies. But international debates, already brisk in the satellite area, can be expected to accelerate.

The International Telecommunications Satellite Program

The joint international commercial venture INTELSAT* began in August 1964. Initially 19 countries agreed to form

* International Telecommunications Satellite Organization.

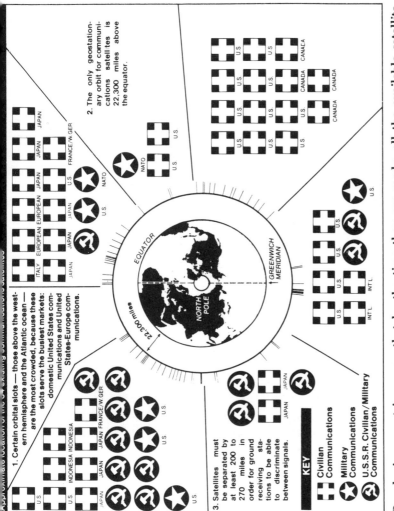

Developing countries worry that by the time they are ready, all the available satellite space will be in use. (From *New York Times*, March 24, 1980. Copyright © 1980 by The New York Times Company. Reprinted by permission.)

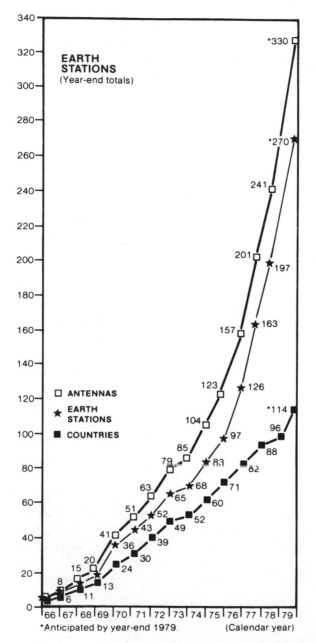

Third world countries eagerly participate in the INTELSAT system, which permits communications with minimal telecommunications infrastructure and leapfrogs them over many previously intractable obstacles. (From INTELSAT Annual Report, 1979. Reprinted by permission.)

a single global communications satellite system using U.S. technology. Now a flourishing international legal entity, INTELSAT has 105 shareholder countries, including most countries outside the Soviet bloc. The USSR has its own communications satellite system, which is ostensibly open to general world membership. In addition to the Eastern European countries, members now include Afghanistan, Vietnam, Cuba, Algeria, and Laos.[2]

INTELSAT handles about two-thirds of all transoceanic communications and links 131 countries and territories through more than 800 direct pathways leading to 239 locally owned earth stations spread around the world. In addition, many member countries are building their own domestic earth stations and using INTELSAT to improve their internal communications. The share of each member country in INTELSAT is based on that country's use of the system, with a minimum share of 0.05 percent. The U.S. participant, COMSAT, held a 23 percent share in 1980, down from 25 percent in 1978.[3]

INTELSAT satellites are stationed in orbits above the equator, 22,300 miles out in space over the Atlantic, Pacific, and Indian Oceans. At this location and altitude, the satellites travel at a speed which, as the earth turns, keeps them stationary in effect or in geosynchronous orbit. They provide telephone, teletype, data, facsimile, and television communications in an area which covers the entire globe. The largest portion of the service—80 percent in 1978—is used for telephone traffic. Television, literally INTELSAT's most visible product, occupies less than 2 percent of INTELSAT capacity.

The communications capacity of satellites is huge and growing. The first INTELSAT V, launched in 1980, carried the equivalent of 12,000 telephone calls and two television programs simultaneously. The projection is for INTELSAT use to double by 1985 and to double again by 1990.[4]

While the single biggest traffic load on INTELSAT is the route between the United States and the United Kingdom—where 2000 circuits are kept busy day and night—the twenty busiest of the earth stations in the system include six in the developing world. These are located in Brazil, Iran, Venezuela, the United Arab Emirates, Singapore, and Argentina. There are many advantages to be had from INTELSAT specifically for developing countries. Among them are the possibility of building at least minimal communications networks without having a prior sophisticated telecommunications infrastructure. In addition, it gives these countries the ability to communicate directly with each other. Previously it was necessary to route their messages through the advanced countries, which in many cases were the former colonial powers who had ruled them.

In 1983, American Telephone and Telegraph (AT&T) plans to launch the first of three Telstar 3 satellites for domestic U.S. communications use. This satellite will carry telephone calls, computer data, facsimile, and television, and will accommodate 21,600 simultaneous telephone conversations. Telstar 3, along with other U.S. satellites, may well be launched by ESA's Ariane.[5]

MARISAT, a joint venture of COMSAT and U.S. International carriers which was begun in 1976, gives satellite services to the U.S. Navy and to commercial shipping and offshore industries. Ships of 35 nations used MARISAT in 1980. By the early 1980s, the International Maritime Satellite Organization (INMARSAT), which had 29 international members in 1980, expects to establish its global system.[6]

While they offer many advantages over cable, for instance, satellites are highly vulnerable to jamming and other forms of interruption, to message interception, and to antisatellite weapons.

Controversial Broadcasting

Compared to the many international advantages which satellites have brought, the disadvantages have thus far been few. Most of the problems which have emerged have been handled in a reasonably cooperative fashion among nations through the International Telecommunication Union (ITU) and within the United Nations Committee on the Peaceful Uses of Outer Space. This latter operates on consensus; that is, when an unanimous decision cannot be reached, the problem is deferred to the next meeting.

But there are two civilian international satellite issues which have such high stakes for so many people that they have been impossible to resolve on either technical or political grounds. These are Direct Broadcasting by Satellite Television (DBS-TV) by individual countries (such as that now being experimented with by Japan domestically) and remote sensing, which is being conducted by the United States, the USSR, and India. Japan and France are planning ambitious operational systems.

DBS-TV, intended for *direct reception* by the *general public*, has occupied a great deal of time in the UN Committee for the Peaceful Uses of Outer Space since 1968.[7] In this as yet experimental system, satellite transmissions of signals can be made strong enough to be picked up by inexpensive antennas placed on the rooftops of individual homes. In Japan, this sort of system, which broadcasts into dishes as small as 18 inches in diameter, is available for about double the cost of an ordinary television set. The problem with DBS-TV is that the transmissions may be from foreign as well as domestic satellites, and the programs being beamed may be comedy shows, news, dramas, music, or they may be propaganda. Thus, DBS-TV technology will permit individuals to watch foreign television programs not necessarily sanctioned by their governments. This has precipitated an international debate over "prior consent."

Briefly, some nations feel that such DBS-TV broadcasts from one country to another without the prior consent of the receiving state is a violation of national sovereignty. During the 1969 annual session of the UN Committee on the Peaceful Uses of Outer Space, the positions of various countries were made clear. The Soviet Union at that time took a stand for prior consent, while the United States opposed it as being contrary to Article 19 of the Universal Declaration of Human Rights and as a threat to the free flow of information. As a result of a joint Swedish-Canadian initiative that same year, an ad hoc group on DBS-TV was formed to consider the technical, legal, and political aspects involved. No consensus was reached, however, for establishing legal instruments to govern DBS-TV.

In 1972, the USSR introduced a proposal to the UN General Assembly for a binding convention of principles for direct television transmission from satellites. The United States strongly opposed this initiative, again citing the threat to free information flow. But the United States was outvoted, 102 to 1, and the General Assembly directed its Committee for Peaceful Uses of Outer Space:[8] ". . . to elaborate principles governing the use by states of artificial earth satellites for direct television broadcasting with a view towards concluding an international agreement or agreements."

This appeared to be a simple conflict between two principles, the free flow of information vs. national sovereignty. But behind this extremely lopsided vote there was also the widely expressed fear that the United States might use its enormous technological advantage for purposes that might not be in the interest of other states.

The United States has said that it has no intention of broadcasting direct television internationally. And the United States has agreed to an ITU radio regulation, which was then reaffirmed in the 1977 plan for satellite broadcasting:[9]

In devising the characteristics of a space station in the broadcasting-satellite service, all technical means available shall be used to reduce to the maximum extent practicable the radiation over the territory of other countries *unless an agreement has been previously reached with such countries.* [Emphasis added]

But this does not change the U.S. rejection of the concept of prior consent. Although many simple compromises, essentially reaffirming the ITU language, have been proposed over the years, no agreement has yet been reached. One argument the United States gives for being so adamant is that the ITU regulation is confined solely to technical matters and has no concern whatsoever with content. Any agreement on content, the United States says, is a form of censorship and thus inconsistent with the First Amendment. This is in line with U.S. arguments in UNESCO on the free flow of information.

On the basis of the free flow of information alone, it is doubtful that the United States could subscribe to the proposed compromise:[10]

A direct television broadcasting service by means of artificial earth satellites specifically directed at a foreign State, which shall be established only when it is not inconsistent with the provision of the relevant instruments of the International Telecommunication Union, shall be based on appropriate agreements and/or arrangements between the broadcasting and receiving States, or the broadcasting entities duly authorized by the respective States, in order to facilitate the freer and wider dissemination of information of all kinds and to encourage co-operation in the field of information and the exchange of information with other countries.

But, like all communications and information matters, the issue is much more complex than at first appears. There is the perception by the United States that free flow of information is under siege, and that compromise on the DBS-TV issue would cut into that. There is also a fear of compromising the U.S. position vis-à-vis international shortwave radio transmission (HF) all over the world, but especially in the USSR. And there is the wish to avoid setting precedents in the area of active and passive military intelligence satellite systems. But probably most important of all, there has been too little political foresight about the suspicions this lonely U.S. position is creating in the general international arena.

Controversial Collecting

The other intractable international satellite problem concerns remote sensing, and for the United States, this means the LANDSAT experimental program. LANDSAT is operated by NASA, and its purpose is to collect data on natural resources on a global basis. The LANDSAT satellites are stationed in polar orbits. This allows them to move around the earth as it turns, measuring the reflection of radio energy from objects on the surface of the earth. Ores and potential petroleum sources, wheat crops, forests, and other agricultural products—even the state of their health—can be discerned, and the condition of coastal zones can be observed. This information is useful for purposes of agricultural land and crop inventory and management, for the management of water resources, for mineral and petroleum exploration, and for other scientific uses.

The United States has from the first followed a principle of open data dissemination and direct foreign participation in the LANDSAT remote sensing program. Everything that has been recorded is published and is available to anyone without political or economic constraint from the Sioux Falls Data Center in South Dakota, which is run by the U.S. Department of Interior. Only the cost of reproduction and processing is charged.

A number of countries, including Canada, Japan, India, Brazil, Italy, Romania, and Sweden, also have collecting stations linked into LANDSAT, and such stations are planned in Africa and Southeast Asia. By mid-1985, this will have grown to fifteen stations, and will encompass most of the earth's surface areas. The cost of such a station, which can be obtained from a number of suppliers in the United States, Canada, Western Europe, and Japan, ranges from $5 to $15 million. The United States charges station owners an annual access fee—currently $200,000—to help offset operations and maintenance costs. It has never tried to recover research and development costs for this project.[11]

The next step for LANDSAT will be the transition from the experimental NASA system to an operational system. The United States has announced its commitment to this, but the technical and management parameters have not yet been defined.[12] This commitment is of great interest and importance to the international community and large investments have been and are being made in overseas facilities to receive, process, and use the data from these U.S. earth resources satellites. At the UN Conference on Science and Technology for Development in 1979 in Vienna, the United States pledged to work with foreign nations to assure systems as compatible and as complementary as possible to theirs, and to work with all data users to make the most of the benefits of this space technology.

Remote sensing is construed by the United States and a large group of other nations as a positive tool to aid in economic and social development, and the collection and dissemination of these data are considered to be fair. Political spokesmen of some countries, especially underdeveloped countries— and these make up about 50 percent of the body of opinion in the UN Committee on the Peaceful Uses of Outer Space— do not agree, however. Or at least they are not happy with the practical results. These countries say they do not want others to peek into their backyards and to know the size and health of their wheat crop before they even know it themselves. They do not want the United States, or their neighbors, or some multinational corporation, to know about mineral resources of which they may not be aware or which they may want to conceal.

In an effort to control this system, they are demanding "prior consent" for remote sensing also. Or at least they feel permission should be obtained from the sensed country before the information is disseminated to third parties.

The argument goes more or less as follows:

Maybe I can't stop you from collecting the information on my country. But I want an international law which says that, having collected it, you can't give it to just anybody who wants it, because you may give it to people whose interests are inimical to mine. This is information which is critical to my national territory—these are my national resources—and I want to control them. As a sovereign, I have the right to control them, and you must respect my sovereignty.

The United States and other countries with sensing capability are, of course, not happy with these demands. Such restrictions would destroy the open nature of the program. So the Swedes and the Canadians have again come up with a compromise proposal. They are suggesting the principle of the right of notification. This, in essence, means that before data is given to a third party, the sensed country must be notified, and that the data must be made available to the sensed country no later than it is given to the third party.

Actually, Argentina and Brazil, who are leaders in the UN debate, have entered into bilateral agreements with the United States, giving access to third parties.

It seems likely that a satisfactory solution will eventually be found, for despite its drawbacks, remote sensing information is very valuable to a large number of people, and an active role is available to a wide variety of participants in this international space activity.

Communications and Information Resources in Development

12

OVER the past several years, various institutional and individual reports and studies have insisted that communications and information resources are essential to development strategies. A comment like this one from a National Academy of Sciences paper is not uncommon:[1]

. . . Improved communications can now help break down rural isolation and promote better education and health care, changes in urban design and more dispersed regional settlement. Recent reductions in costs and improvements in performance indicate that improved communications technologies could become a major new force in development.

An Agency for International Development (AID) report to the U.S. Congress echos the thought:[2]

Communications systems are a crucial part of the economic and social infrastructure of modern nations; developing countries need technical assistance, both to modernize their internal communications systems and to establish links with global and possibly regional systems. . . .

And yet, communications and information is one of the most neglected areas of development aid.

There is almost no translation of such statements into budgetary provisions for communications and information infrastructure building. AID's contribution to communications was about $27 million in 1978, of which more than half went to one country, Egypt. In 1979, this increased to about $35 million. The International Communications Agency (ICA) spends about $1.2 million, or about 3.2 percent of a total $373 million budget for development. The Export-Import (EXIM) Bank devotes only about 3.8 percent of its annual loans to this area.[3]

The $82 million which the World Bank allocates to communications purposes is approximately 2.5 percent of its total loan budget. In the period from 1949 to 1978—29 years— the World Bank lent a measly $1.7 billion for communications, an average of about $56 million a year.[4]

The World Bank is very interested in financing institution building, and in helping to facilitate efficient and equitable national economic growth. Thus, it says, to the extent that the lack of communications and information is "a primary constraint to sector growth," it will consider limited loans in this area. The Bank stresses, however, that it is a lender of last resort. The problem is that there is no lender of first resort.

Upon his retirement as World Bank President in October 1980, Robert McNamara took the United States to task for not doing more to support the Bank in its overall development work. In relation to per capita or to total income, the United States devotes roughly only one-half as much money to development as any other industrialized country except Italy, despite the fact that the developing countries are the biggest export market the United States has. This is a market bigger than that in Western Europe, Eastern Europe, the Soviet

Union, and China combined, he noted, and said that if the United States fails to assist these countries economically, it is only hurting itself. The newly rich OPEC countries, developing countries themselves, give more support to the World Bank than does the United States in relation to their size, population, and income, he pointed out.[5]

The poor showing in communications and information and development is not confined to official aid or to the international financial institutions. Investment by the developing countries themselves in this area has been running at about .3 percent of their Gross Domestic Product (GDP). This is less than half the average annual percentage of GDP devoted by developed countries, which have major communications plants already in place. As a result, the developing countries' share of the world's telephones is even less than their share of world income. In 1976, developing countries, with 71 percent of the world's population and 19 percent of its income, had only 7 percent of its telephones.[6]

Handsome profits could be realized by private enterprise under the right circumstances in the area of *urban* telecommunications in developing countries. And governments could hope to recoup their investments here. But rural network building cannot at this time offer profit incentive to such private investors.

There are, of course, exceptions to this dismal picture. Two major ones are Egypt and Saudi Arabia. Egypt has signed a contract for $1.8 billion with a European consortium to repair its telecommunications network and to modernize it for the development period 1980–1984. Saudi Arabia is spending $7 billion to bring a modern telephone system to its towns and villages rapidly. Ten thousand telephones are being installed in Saudi Arabia each month. When the program began in 1977, only seven Saudi cities had telephone services to one another, and this was via only 150,000 phones. Twenty-seven months later, eighty-four cities and villages had been connected by 750,000 phones, and the Saudis are now convinced that their goal of two million phones is not going to be enough.[7]

A desert telephone booth. (From *Time*, February 23, 1981). (Reprinted by permission of Woodfin Camp.)

Communications as Political Dynamite

What are the expressed reasons for not supporting communications and information in the area of development? In the main, there are five:

1. There is no existent infrastructure to receive it.
2. Communications and information systems are extremely capital intensive.
3. The economic benefits of communications and information have not been proven.
4. It may not benefit the poorest of the poor.
5. It benefits only urban areas and the elites.

But there is a sixth reason, which is rarely expressed.

6. Communications and information is political dynamite.

In support of Reason 1, the World Bank says that it is not just a matter of funds:[8]

. . . by far the most important [constraint] is the lack in many instances of an adequate organizational or institutional structure in the telecommunications sector, on both a countrywide basis and within the telecommunications operating entities themselves. This may seem like an unusual statement to be made in a paper concerned with the financing of telecommunications, but it seems that in many instances, if the major institutional and organizational problems were resolved, many of the financial, technical and manpower problems would essentially resolve themselves.

It is true that the lack of basic infrastructures may be crucial. In 1977, the United States loaned an experimental communications satellite to India for educational purposes, which tied the broadcasting facilities of that country to about 2400 villages. A total population of about 20 million Indians was reached through the experiment with entertainment, cultural programs, and news mixed with public health and agricultural education programs. After a year of educating the Indian farmer in the necessity to rotate his crops, to use improved types of seeds, and to fertilize lavishly, grave shortages of fertilizer and seeds and difficulties with the supply system to the villages became apparent.

This is illustrative of the staggering complexity which is encountered at multiple levels of development. Communications creates other demands which must be planned for. And communications alone may simply exaggerate other shortages and generate expectations which cannot be met.

Regarding Reason 2, that communications and information is very capital intensive, it is true that a modern communications system is a matter of investing billions of dollars. But where to get even a start on these billions? AID has not supported capital investment in telecommunications since 1962, that is, since the beginning of supermodern telecommunications.[9]

About Reason 3, that the economic benefits of communications and information have not been proven, the World Bank says:[10]

The reasons for this (non-investment in telecommunications infrastructure) revolve around the fact that the ultimate economic benefits and real priority of investment in telecommunications in a developing country are hard to identify *with precision* . . . [Emphasis added]

This argument is made not only by the World Bank but also by other official aid givers and sometimes by developing country governments themselves. If it is "precise data" we are waiting for, then pity the poor developing countries.

The following chart shows the relationship between the number of telephones per hundred inhabitants of a country and that country's GDP per capita.

That there is a relationship between high GDP and high numbers of telephones and low GDP and low numbers of telephones is unmistakable. But here one gets involved in the old chicken and egg argument—which came first, the

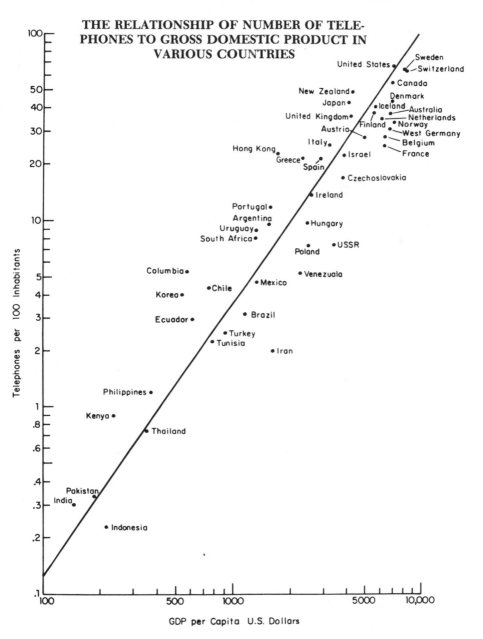

THE RELATIONSHIP OF NUMBER OF TELEPHONES TO GROSS DOMESTIC PRODUCT IN VARIOUS COUNTRIES

Which came first: the money or the telephone? (From INTELTRADE, December 15, 1979. Based on Siemen's 1979 data. Reprinted by permission.)

money or the telephone? The argument has often been made that it was the former. But John F. Magee, President of Arthur D. Little, Inc., argued convincingly before the McGovern Committee Hearings in June 1977 that this was no longer believed to be the case.[11]

Reason 4, that communications and information may not benefit the poorest of the poor, is a valid one. Increasingly, national and international official aid efforts are being aimed at the lowest 40 percent income group of a given nation. And the forty or so very poorest countries are the chief aid recipients today. The Carter administration strategy for this sort of aid to the poorest of the poor was called the Basic Human Needs program. It concentrated on health care, food, rural development, and other basic needs for survival.

When people live in utter deprivation, there is definitely a serious question of whether telecommunications, television, and other communications and information-related projects are indeed of the highest priority. But it can also be asked whether these people will ever live in any other way if communications and information resources are denied them. This is a matter which deserves the most careful study.

If viewed from the perspective of the Basic Human Needs strategy, then the argument that communications and information resources will benefit only the urban areas and the elites, Reason 5, also has at least a certain immediate validity. But urban centers cannot be dismissed out of hand. In developing as in developed countries, urban centers have played an all-important role in nation building since the early Middle Ages. The dangers inherent in mass rural migrations to the cities notwithstanding, people have flocked and will continue to flock into the world's cities in an effort to improve their lives. But if their expectations cannot be met in some way, then the urban centers become the foci of revolutions. Thus, to make the cities of developing countries functional and livable would appear to be a prime development goal, and one at least as important as the development of rural areas. Urban centers are also the centers of commerce, without which there

is no money. And without money there can be no development, and thus there will always be millions or billions of
the poorest of the poor.

While it is true that the elites may siphon off more than
their share of urban improvements, it is also true that elites
come in many stripes. Among them are, of course, the people
who must lead their developing nations. But they must have
resources with which to lead them.

Telecommunications is a basic ingredient of commerce and
business. An Aspen Institute report makes this point:[12] " . . .
The key feature of a modern economy is close coordination
between the various productive units. . . . Without a reliable,
cheap, and widespread system of communications, coordination becomes an impossible task." And then it adds the under-
statement: "The information infrastructure—postal system,
telephone system, the media—has not been construed as an
essential precondition for economic take-off."

Reason 6 could be where "it's really at." Communications
and information is political dynamite. Communications and
information is a powerful instrument for political development and political change. The governments most in need
of communications and information in their development programs are perhaps the least anxious for massive upsets. Mrs.
Ghandi is alleged to have said, during her first period of emergency rule: "A refrigerator seen on a comedy television show
can become a revolutionary symbol to the deprived villager."
The rulers of the most needy nations may not be willing to
rock the boat.

To the extent that governments of developing countries
are interested in communications and information, they do
tend to focus on point-to-point urban business links which
have direct economic payoffs and reach relatively few people.
Some governments even make it a point to avoid mass media
communications by television or radio. Other governments
want to develop communications and information to extend
central administrative control, or to foster a common language
or value or culture. Or they may wish to nurture the desired

political expression. Some leaders of some countries see communications as a means of imposing central police powers, stifling dissent, and improving internal security.

The boundary between the elevating and suppressing aims of communications uses is a very slim one, and is frequently complex, confused, and difficult to discern. The choices for both the donor and the recipient governments are profound and fundamental.

The social consequences of communications and information are enormous, and perhaps more important, they are almost impossible to predict or to direct. What does it mean when people in isolated villages begin to communicate with each other, with the county seat, the provincial seat, or the capital for the first time? What happens when access to transistors and tape recorders and television occurs suddenly, and peoples receive news and other messages from sources until then denied? What are the consequences of sudden exposure to new political ideas? Of becoming suddenly politically interested? What are the consequences, and for whom?

It has been pointed out that 90 percent of the developing nations receiving loans are:[13] " . . . moving in ways that are clearly contributing to a peaceful world. . . ." But that the recipient may bite the hand that feeds it cannot be denied as a probability. Iran could be a classic example for study. We know that communications and information played a major role in the execution of the 1979 revolution in that country.[14] But what went on before that time? It would be fascinating to know the correlation between the introduction of communications and information resources into Iran and the rise of disaffection for the Shah. It is not too ridiculous even to hypothesize that the Shah was not brought down because he "modernized too fast," or "bought expensive military toys while the people starved," or even that he offended the religious components of the country. But rather, that he fell because he gave the Iranian people the communications and information resources which permitted them to know what they lacked, and gave them the means to express their will.

Certainly new communications and information facilities led various elements of Iranian society to discover their common discontent with the Shah's rule, although often for diverse and contradictory reasons. Therefore, it could be said that, despite all his dictatorial principles and practices, what the Shah de facto accomplished was the democratization of the peoples of Iran.

On examination, it can be seen that the engineering required for communications and information and development is difficult but not insurmountable. Doubtless, the money could be found someplace. And the economic benefits of communications and information to development can certainly be said to be highly suggestive. A more important problem may be that we have today a generation of long-range planners in the developing countries whose training in development strategies (for the most part in Western schools) did not take communications and information considerations into account.

Electronic Security and Defense Systems, Including Command, Control, Communications, and Intelligence (C³I)

13

THE electronic warfare equipment business in the United States—communications and information devices and systems for national security and defense purposes—has grown from about a $500 million industry in 1974 to a $3.5 billion industry in 1980. This figure is expected to reach $5.7 billion by 1983.[1] This is not an industry which the U.S. can choose to support or not to support. It is one many say *must* be supported to maintain military parity with the Soviet Union.

While radio communications and signal intelligence played an important role in World War I, the use of radar during World War II's Battle of Britain marked the real beginning of today's sophisticated communications and information-based defense systems. The detection of enemy aircraft, the careful ground control, the instructions from the ground to airborne pilots, and operational research to focus defense strategy, all foreshadowed an event of under-reported significance over southern Lebanon in 1979. There, Israeli-flown American-made F-15s and Syrian-flown Soviet MIG 21s met twice—for two or three minutes.[2]

Unlike their World War II counterparts, modern fighters must carry not only electronic equipment which gives them the information to take the offensive, but also defensive equipment which can jam radar, obliterate tracking signals so that missiles cannot "see" the plane, and misdirect missiles by deceptive signals. United States technological superiority over that of the USSR in the above-cited instance seemed reassured when five MIGs were downed while all F-15s returned safely to base.

The cost of electronic gear, excluding actual weapons, represents about 30 to 40 percent of the total cost of today's fighter planes.[3] This gear must be significantly updated four or five times during the life span of the plane, indicating the rapidity of technological change and the equal rapidity of obsolescence in the communications and information field.

The Nuclear Defense Nervous System

Command, Control, and Communications is the command system which keeps U.S. forces under the direct control of the President or the National Command Authority (NCA)* during prenuclear crises and during and in the aftermath of actual nuclear conflict. Because of the danger that nonnuclear crises involving U.S. forces may escalate to a nuclear exchange, these crises are also included in this system. Signal and electronic intelligence furnishes the bulk of data for today's intelligence analyses. Together, Command, Control, Communications, and Intelligence are known by the acronym C³I.

This nervous system of our national defense is an electronic communications and information system. It includes the various commercial telecommunications networks. In fact, most of the day-to-day communication within the U.S. military and

* The National Command Authority is the President and his authorized successors.

the government, both inside the United States and, to a lesser extent, internationally, is conducted through commercial channels.

The strategic policy objectives of the United States require that this country be prepared to fight, if necessary, a protracted nuclear war. To support the conduct of such a war, C³I must be able to perform many functions. Among these are to:[4]

- Provide timely warning of nuclear attack and an accurate assessment of the nature and extent of such an attack when it has occurred.
- Provide for the survival of the National Command Authority (NCA).
- Maintain communications between NCA and the nuclear forces.
- Monitor the execution of decisions.
- Assess the results of such execution.
- Reconstitute and redirect surviving nuclear forces.

And, when the time comes to terminate the conflict, the capability of NCA must have remained intact, and the C³I system must be able to command an ending to operations and, presumably, to help pick up the pieces.

Especially difficult psychological problems are presented by the necessity to provide timely warning of nuclear attack. The then Director for Indications and Warnings in the Office of the Assistant Secretary of Defense said in 1978:[5]

Given that the probability is high that we will ignore the information assembled from our national technical intelligence sources which indicates that the other side really intends to go to war, tactical warning needs to be highly credible to overcome the mindset that says, "It cannot really happen; we have got it all under control in the political environment." To be highly credible, tactical warning must answer what it is, who did it, are we the subject of the attack, when was it initiated, and, of course, when will it arrive.

This is quite an order when the *maximum* estimated time available for reaction to a missile attack launched from the

Soviet Union is thirty minutes, and only ten minutes if it is launched off the coast of the United States by enemy submarines. Accuracy of information and the elimination of errors is thus a key goal.

There are basically two types of errors in warning systems: false negatives and false positives. In a false negative, a launch goes undetected and could lead to an attack with no forewarning. This could be caused by malfunctioning detection equipment or by enemy jamming or blinding of sensors. In a false positive, a launch is "detected" that has not occurred, and this could lead to a counterattack for no reason.

Unfortunately, within a few months' span in 1980, the United States had at least three false positive alarms. That is, three came to the attention of the American public. In each instance, warplanes and missile forces were alerted. In each instance, through human judgment and using backup devices, the error of the warning was detected within ten minutes. Allegedly, in none of these instances was the President or other senior political figure in the government alerted. Thus, had the alarm been bona fide, ten precious minutes would have been lost.

After extensive investigation of the last such false alarm, on June 6, 1980—the second to occur within one week—senior Pentagon officials proudly disclosed that it was the failure of a small electronic component that had twice sent bomber crews hurriedly to start their plane engines, put missile crews in a high state of readiness, and informed submarines to respond to possible nuclear attack.[6]

These false alerts, rightly, caused worldwide shock waves, since it was not just Americans who were endangered.

False alarms become even more important in light of recent military thinking which suggests that planners foresee a time when they will have only moments for decision making. Thus, they are talking about a "launch on warning" strategy. This, as a *New York Times* editorial put it, means: "Strike when that 46 cent circuit begins to quiver."

The Economist (London)[7] and many international newspapers also expressed great alarm. The *New York Times*[7] recalled a saying that goes:

> *For want of a nail, the shoe was lost*
> *For want of a shoe, the horse was lost*
> *For want of a horse, the kingdom was lost.*

In the cases cited, it was human judgment that prevailed, and that is the way it should be. But one must be aware that this is the case. Electronic equipment, communications systems, and computers do what people tell them to do. And they are only as strong as their weakest links. And yet, these vulnerable pieces of equipment have been made the chief assistants to individual military commanders, to the President of the United States, and to his closest aides.

Backseat Driving and Other Pitfalls

While C³I is an integral part of nuclear crisis management it is, fortunately, used more frequently for various less dramatic present-day international crises. Such crises have historically had a way of getting out of hand, which can no longer be tolerated in a nuclear age. So, now that we have such sophisticated communications means in place, decisions are rarely left to the discretion of the regional or local commander. Shortly after an alert, the President, or the Secretary of Defense, personally takes control of the situation. Whether this is either necessary or desirable can be debated, but it is a fact created by the nuclear and the information age.

The necessity for a secure C³I system that works under diverse conditions worldwide is illustrated by the following cases.

The case of the *USS Liberty*, had it not been so serious, could be racked up as a comedy of communications errors. On June 8, 1967, during the Arab-Israeli war, that ship was cruising 12 miles off the Sinai peninsula. It was there for the specific purpose of eavesdropping on battlefield communications. During a period of thirteen hours, six urgent messages for the *Liberty* were sent out by the Pentagon, ordering that ship out of the area and to a point 100 miles offshore.

None of the messages reached the ship in time. Two were misrouted to a U.S. communications station in the Philippines. One went to Greece. One message was never directed to the *Liberty*. One was lost in the electronic labyrinth at the Army Communications Station at Pirmasens, Germany. A final message, marked URGENT and TOP SECRET by the Joint Chiefs of Staff, spent the morning of June 8th:[8] " . . . being passed from ship to ship and from communication station to communication station in search of a circuit to *Liberty* that was cleared for TOP SECRET traffic. Finding no such circuit, the message went undelivered."

The message contained was of a "run for your life" variety.

The result of this series of human and computer errors was tragic. At two in the afternoon, Israeli planes and boats began a coordinated attack on the *Liberty* with gunfire, torpedos, rockets, and napalm which lasted for an hour and twenty minutes. At the end of the attack, 34 U.S. sailors were dead and 171 wounded.

The incident of the U.S. intelligence ship *Pueblo*, which was attacked by the North Koreans in 1968, is another instance of failed communications. The National Security Agency had notified the Pentagon more than two days beforehand that an attack on the *Pueblo* was likely. But again, due to a variety of command and administrative snafus, the ship was not notified. The ship, its men, and highly classified information and information equipment were, as a result, captured by the North Koreans.

Here, not only was a physical disaster and a tragedy for the ship's men witnessed, but this was also the first instance ever, in the history of the United States, of a Navy ship being hijacked on the high seas.[9]

Sometimes the problem is too much information. During the evacuation of the American Embassy in Saigon in 1975, very good communications were maintained throughout. That is, the United States had very good, unsecured voice communications with the Embassy and were apprised of every detail. And so were the North Vietnamese.[10]

Another instance of this sort was the *Mayaguez* incident of 1976. In this case, the ship had been highjacked by the Cambodians, and President Ford had decided to retake it by force. Communications worked perfectly, and the President himself had direct control. However, everything that was discussed was discussed in the open. There is good reason to believe that the Cambodians were listening and knew every detail of exactly what was going to occur. For example, when helicopters were sent in to take the island where the ship was anchored, the direct orders for so doing were passed from the U.S. Air Force to the U.S. Navy—over open circuits. Thus, how many helicopters and how many men would participate, where they were going, at what time, and the replenishment rate were all open secrets, and the United States did all the work for the Cambodian military intelligence. Twenty U.S. marines were killed during this operation.[11]

These are just some of the problems which are cropping up with the new uses of communications for command and control. Unless communications can be secured, would we not, in fact, be better off without them? And what is the real price in terms of readiness and morale of area commanders of being short-circuited by the President or the Pentagon? The day will doubtless arrive when several flashpoints will occur simultaneously, and it will not be practical to conduct operations from Washington. Whatever the costs, it is unlikely that responsibilities and decision-making powers will ever revert back to the local scene. This has vast implications, the full impact of which has yet to be considered.

Notwithstanding an unclassified Joint Chiefs of Staff after-the-fact critique of the rescue operation, the details of C^3I's role during the failed rescue attempt of the U.S. hostages in Iran are still swathed in secrecy.[12] But we know that there was presidential contact, and that the President made the final decision to abort the mission. What happened in between at some of the critical decision points we do not yet know. But we will eventually know, and it should make fascinating reading.

United States communications, navigational, and intelligence satellites and other electronic communications and information equipment and systems are all themselves highly vulnerable to electronic warfare measures. This includes jamming, antisatellite weapons, and sabotage. They are also constantly prey to simple breakdown.

Notwithstanding the importance of these electronic systems to U.S. defenses, and their vulnerability, few policymakers in the Defense Department, the State Department, or the National Security Council have any real appreciation of their complexity. There is virtual ignorance among the general members of these bodies—including many senior military officers—of the strengths and weaknesses of these technologies and systems, and of what they can and cannot do. And there is an almost total unawareness of the nature and workings of the vast domestic industrial complex which underlies, interacts with, and gives these systems life support. This lack of understanding results in ignoring of their potential, in deep skepticism and distrust of electronic defenses, or—what is probably the worst—in overreliance on these systems as miracle workers.

From the earliest days of military conflict, it has been dogma that commanding officers must know their men. Extrapolated to modern warfare, the people who must rely on electronic defenses in crisis situations must understand them from the time their programs are written, and through every step of their development and use.

It should be stressed that the concepts and architecture of electronic defense systems were developed in an era of U.S. strategic superiority. In the current environment of, at best, strategic parity, some of the basic underlying concepts may be outdated and should be reexamined and strengthened.

How do the Soviets do in the electronic defense systems area? According to American and NATO authorities, they do very well. Command and control, especially of their air force and navies, is deeply ingrained in the power structure of the USSR. Many authorities give the Soviets a clear advantage in the area of secure communications, and a standoff as far as electronic warfare itself is concerned. Former Secretary of the Navy J. William Middendorf has said that:[13] "The Soviets have the best command and control one can imagine."

Perhaps the most important lesson the United States can learn is that Soviet military commanders, during their periods of training and assignments, are said to have been subjected to many more communications and related problems than have their American counterparts. They are thus reported to have a very much greater familiarity with the nature, the mission, and the limitations of the systems with which they have to deal. In effect, this could be more important than highly sophisticated arrays of gadgetry. And even if this image of the Soviet military commander should prove exaggerated, it would not hurt the United States to try to emulate it.

Arms Control and the Role of Communications and Information in Peacekeeping

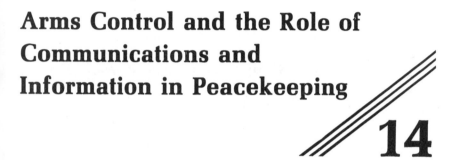

14

THE 1979 Senate Salt II Treaty ratification debates centered in large part on the adequacy of U.S. spy satellites, electronic monitoring, telemetry data, and other kinds of intelligence intercepts to verify points of agreement between the United States and the Soviet Union. "National means of verification" was indeed the central concept of this treaty, which has been shelved due to international crises in Cuba, Iran, and Afghanistan. This international treaty, like Salt I, proposed to give legitimacy to the use of communications and information resources by a foreign power in outer space for technical intelligence operations over the territory of another sovereign state. In other words, there was a gentleman's agreement between the two parties to permit each other, under certain conditions, to spy.

The 1972 Salt I Treaty, then dealing with limitations on antiballistic missile (ABM) systems, made the following provisions:[1]

- Each party shall use national technical means of verification at its disposal consistent with generally recognized principles of international law. . . .
- That each party undertakes not to interfere with the national technical means of verification of the other party. . . .
- And that each party undertakes not to use deliberate concealment measures which impede verification by national technical means.

Until relatively recently, intelligence operations were mainly carried out using human collectors of information, and these are, of course, still heavily employed. During World War II, aerial photographs began to be extensively taken and operations planned based on the information provided. A classic example of this was the detection and bombing of the German Peenemunde V-2 plants. But technical intelligence reconnaisance truly came of age in the late 1950s with the technology embodied in the U-2 airplane.

This high-flying U.S. aircraft with a camera capable of taking pictures from 80,000 feet permitted analysts to recognize objects on the ground with dimensions as small as 12 inches.

The results prompted the effusive statement:[2]

This technical near miracle revolutionized intelligence collection, eventually rivaling signals for producing voluminous details about foreign areas and reducing the burden on the secret agent enormously. It also gave the analyst historical depth and evidence, permitting researchers to identify lead time traces in weapons development once new radars, missiles, aircraft, submarines, etc., had been discovered. . . .

But along with this technical intelligence breakthrough came the shattering of the politics of denial, which was an engrained feature of intelligence and foreign affairs activities. When Gary Powers was shot down over the USSR in his U-2 in 1960, the reaction attempted by the White House was routine. President Eisenhower denied categorically any knowledge of the existence of either a U-2 plane or a pilot named Gary Powers. But, unfortunately, both were captured alive and well by the Soviets. Within a few days, the Eisenhower Administration was forced to admit that the United States had been spying for some time over Soviet territory. And thus a new open chapter in an ultrasecret area was written.[3]

President Eisenhower may already have had something like U-2s in mind when, at the Summit Conference in 1955—the "Spirit of Geneva" conference—he proposed an open skies mutual inspection pact which would limit the arms race, based on aerial reconnaissance of each other's territories. This was rejected out of hand by then Soviet Premier Khrushchev. But as capabilities for intelligence satellites proliferated in both the United States and the USSR and for a long time neither party was able to destroy the other's satellites, these mutual inspections came into being. This de facto situation was then made de jure with Salt I.

Spies in the Skies

The United States uses two types of photoreconnaissance satellites. One is a scanning satellite with low resolution cameras covering wide areas for general monitoring. The other, a much higher resolution system, focuses very advanced cameras on specific targets of interest. The scanning camera data is usually transmitted telemetrically to ground stations, while the film canisters from the high resolution system are deorbited on command and recovered in midair by Air Force transport planes.

Congressman Les Aspin described this activity in 1979:[4]

. . . U.S. surveillance satellites currently provide complete photographic coverage of the USSR at frequent intervals. If suspicions are aroused by the regular large area survey photographs, "close look" cameras can be ordered to rephotograph the area in question, providing more detailed information. The present generation of high resolution cameras on U.S. surveillance satellites are theoretically capable of making a clear photograph of an object one foot across from an altitude of 100 miles. . . .

. . . U.S. satellites . . . are now equipped with multispectral sensors that can penetrate camouflage and can also observe nighttime activity. Infrared sensors are particularly good at detecting underground missile silos and silos that have been camouflaged. . . .

Defense Secretary Harold Brown testified in detail before Congress in support of Salt II ratification, saying that the United States is now able to monitor Soviet missile testing from space, aircraft, and ships, and from land-based radar:[5]

We monitor missile test firings with a wide variety of sensors; cameras taking pictures of launch and impact areas; infrared detectors measuring heat from the engines; radars tracking ICBMs in flight; and radios receiving Soviet telemetry signals. . . . The use of multiple sources complicates any effort to disguise or conceal violations. In the course of twenty to thirty tests of the new ICBM, we collect thousands of reels of magnetic tape and spend tens of thousands of hours processing, analyzing, and correlating this vast array of data. . . .

A Rand study also expressed confidence in the ability of these communications and information systems to effectively provide the information which would ensure that Soviet arms capabilities could not be secretly stepped up. Among others, Secretary of State Vance testified that the U.S. technological capabilities for the verification of Salt II were adequate. Salt I was not signed until the United States was sure that its communications and information technologies were up to the task of strategic arms monitoring.[6]

A further step in the uses of communications and information resources for monitoring arms buildups was taken when Secretary of State Kissinger, during his shuttle diplomacy, worked out an arrangement for technical assistance by the United States for peacekeeping in the Sinai. The following

MAP OF THE SINAI PEACEKEEPING AREA

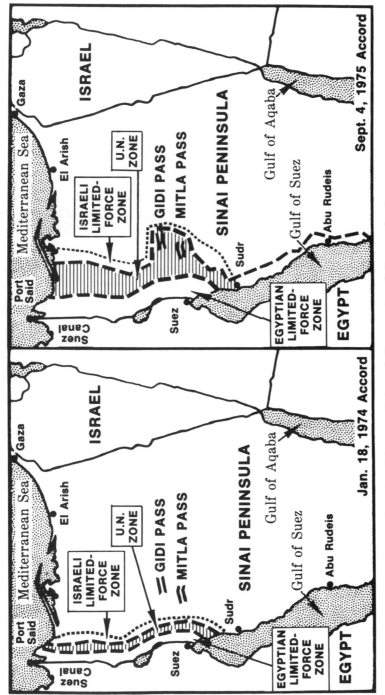

Reprinted by permission of *Congressional Quarterly, Inc.*

map shows the area in question. The U.S. proposal, attached
to the agreement between Egypt and Israel, initialed on September 1, 1975, in Jerusalem and Alexandria and signed in
Geneva on September 4, read partially as follows:[7]

1. The Early Warning system . . . shall have the following elements:
   a. There shall be two surveillance stations to provide strategic
   early warning, one operated by Egyptian and one operated
   by Israeli personnel. Their locations are shown on the map
   attached to the Basic Agreement. Each station shall be
   manned by not more than 250 technical and administrative
   personnel. They shall perform the functions of visual and
   electronic surveillance only within their stations.
   b. In support of these stations, to provide tactical early warning
   and to verify access to them, three watch stations shall be
   established by the United States in the Mitla and Giddi
   Passes as . . . shown on the map. . . . These stations shall
   be operated by United States civilian personnel. *In support
   of these stations, there shall be established three unmanned
   electronic sensor fields at both ends of each Pass and in
   the general vicinity of each station and the roads leading
   to and from those stations.* [Emphasis added]

The duties of the United States civilian personnel, who were
not to total more than 200, were to:

. . . verify the nature of the operations of the stations and all movement into and out of each station and . . . immediately report any
detected divergency from its authorized role of visual and electronic
surveillance to the Parties to the Basic Agreement (Egypt and Israel)
and to the United Nations Emergency Force.

This, together with U.S. aerial reconnaissance already in
operation over the area, bolstered confidence against surprise
attack sufficiently to permit disengagement in the Sinai. This
plan, which was put into operation immediately, has been
extremely successful and is still contributing to stability in

that area. Speaking to the United Nations in 1978, Vice President Mondale dubbed this use of electronics devices "the eyes and ears of peace."[8] He expressed U.S. willingness to consider similar requests from other countries with like peacekeeping needs.

The status quo is never maintained for long in the rapidly changing field of communications and information technologies. Any advance in an intelligence interception device, for instance, swiftly leads to a counter device on the other side. Both superpowers are now devoting great resources to developing antisatellite systems. Constant attention is therefore necessary, both in the area of research and development, to maintain technological superiority, and in the area of diplomacy, to adapt to political shifts.

The loss of the telemetry and other electronic listening posts in Iran after that revolution was a serious blow to U.S. national means of verification and to U.S. defense systems. Other stations worldwide could become equally vulnerable at any time. More countries—France and Japan—are expected to have reconnaissance satellites in the near future. China, in a limited way, is already in the game. Thus, the monopoly formerly held by the United States and the Soviet Union, broken in the civilian operational satellite systems area, has been broken in the national security satellite field as well.

The equilibrium which has been established between the United States and the Soviet Union in the area of arms control is a very delicate one, and requires constant observation and adjustment. But national technical means of verification promises to be a versatile tool for many future uses. Its potential is just beginning to be recognized on both technical and political fronts.

The Widening Role of Electronic Codes, Message Interception, and Message Protection

15

SIGNAL security (COMSEC)—the coding and other ways of securing U.S. government messages for transmission—and signal intelligence (SIGINT)—the interception and decoding of the messages of others by the U.S. government—are both National Security Agency activities.[1]

COMSEC activities have been described as including:[2]

. . . all ways of keeping secret both human messages, such as telegrams and telephone conversations, and electronic messages such as computer to computer data exchanges. These ways include cryptography—varied techniques for putting the messages into secret form by code or cipher; the elements of the message—letters, electronic pulses, voice sounds—can be scrambled or replaced by other elements. The receiver, who must know the key or secret procedure used in encryption, then reverses the process to read the original message. . . .

The activities included in SIGINT are:[2]

. . . all methods of extracting information from transmissions. These methods can include identifying radars or translating telemetered data of intercontinental ballistic missiles in flight. Other methods deal largely with human communications. Among these are interception of messages in plain languages; traffic analysis, which matches radio call signs to particular military or other headquarters and draws inferences from the volume of traffic on various radio circuits; and cryptanalysis, which breaks codes or ciphers that armor messages . . .

Everything having to do with signal security and intelligence is of the utmost sensitivity, and there are stiff penalties by all governments for those found guilty of releasing such information to potential or actual adversaries or even to the merely unauthorized.

These matters are indeed so sensitive that U.S. and German cryptographers did not compare World War II notes until thirty-four years later. When they did, American descriptions of how Allied convoys located and avoided German U-boats, how clues were obtained about German V weapons, and how dispatches by the Japanese Ambassador to Berlin to his government in Tokyo were intercepted and read, made it clear that the war was significantly shortened by the Allied ability to break codes.

With advances in interception and communications technologies, however, it is becoming harder and harder to maintain secrecy or to keep this specialized knowledge confined to small government intelligence agencies. With its many possible new uses, cryptology now not only plays an extensive role in intelligence and security but also has a prominent part in diplomatic activity. Its heavy use leads, in turn, to disclosure through political and military events. The *USS Maddox* encounter with North Vietnamese patrol boats in the Gulf of Tonkin in 1964, as well as the previously described Israeli attack on the *USS Liberty* in 1967 and the North Korean capture of the *USS Pueblo* in 1968, each revealed to the world at large some of the intercept techniques the United States is using.

The uses of cryptology have now been openly cited and legitimized in formal international agreements. The stalled Salt II disarmament arrangement with the Soviet Union specifies that in certain instances, the parties will mutually abstain from its use:[3] ". . . Neither party shall engage in deliberate denial of telemetric information such as through the use of encryption whenever such denial impedes verification of compliance with the provisions of the treaty. . . ."

This is, of course, like most diplomatic arrangements, of necessity ambiguous. When, then, *is* encryption permissible? When does encryption interfere with verification, and when does it not? How much interference is acceptable? And, most importantly, who will make these decisions?

If You Don't Want It Known, Don't Use the Phone

The various uses to which cryptology must be, should be, and could be put are now emerging from the closet. Like other technological advances—those in atomic energy, for example—encryption has been the spur to public debate.

There are basically three different areas of intelligence activity involved in these debates. It is good to differentiate these, even if the lines are not neatly drawn. They are:

1. Signal intelligence directed by governments toward foreign government activities. The usual protection of military and diplomatic secrets is involved here.

2. Government intelligence directed toward the civilian activities of other countries. This has always been included in cloak and dagger activities, but has enormously increased.

3. Nongovernmental intelligence activities directed toward other civilian activities, both domestically and internationally. This includes the spying by businesses on each other's trade secrets and the threats to the privacy and confidentiality of the messages of individuals.

There has been a virtual explosion of activities in all three of these areas as a consequence of new communications and information technologies and uses. Many problems in the first area can be inferred from earlier discussions.

Because it is cheaper, quicker, and more efficient, today's business is conducted less and less by letter and more and more by telephone. Thus the conventional protected route of the United States first class mail system is being bypassed. In addition, the widespread use of data communications from computer to computer over telephone lines has sprung up. This means large amounts of data which used to remain in a fixed spot are now more often in transit. Meanwhile, since 1950, the telephone company has been using microwave transmission for long-distance switched telephone services because it is much cheaper than underground cable. Today, more than 70 percent of all long-distance toll-call mileage within the United States is said to be conducted by microwave.

Microwave transmissions are unfortunately considerably easier to access by unauthorized parties than are underground cables. They can be accessed from distances up to 5 or 10 miles, and the accessor has a choice of thousands of calls. Businesses are thus finding it necessary to protect themselves against "snooping" on their telephone traffic by—among others—foreign nations.

In 1975, the Rockefeller Commission on Central Intelligence Agency Activities reported that the Soviets were monitoring "millions" of domestic U.S. telephone conversations of both businesses and private individuals. President Carter has acknowledged that:[4] "Within the last number of years, because of the radio transmission of telephone conversations, the intercept on a passive basis of these kinds of transmissions has become a common ability for nations to pursue."

Why would a foreign power wish to listen to your call to the pediatrician, or your boring conversation with your Aunt Harriet? The answer is that it doesn't and it doesn't have to. To sift out the few wanted telephone calls from the thousands of unwanted ones, the "snooper" simply uses the computer, which can be programmed to count the clicks and beeps. The computer then compares the beeps of the originating and/or called numbers with those it has been instructed to monitor, and then records the conversations desired.

This spying activity directed toward civilians is mainly aimed at obtaining commercial, financial, and scientific information. In today's world, this may be worth as much as the most weighty diplomatic dispatch, or for that matter, many military secrets. According to an East German defector, economic espionage to the tune of $2.8 million dollars saves East German industry an annual $170 million in research and development costs.[5] Thus, under the aegis of advanced communications, the industry of the United States is inadvertently giving away what it ought to be selling. Such snoops also look for information warning of an energy crisis or a dollar crisis, which can be extraordinarily important to them.

When a foreign state spies on the U.S. civilian sector, one remedy would be for the President either to kick the offender out of the country or tell that offender's country to cease and desist and make it stick. But the President, with the indirect concurrence of the Congress, says more or less "forget it," because the U.S. government also wants to spy on foreign data.

Microwave must move in a direct line, and cannot penetrate or bend around geographic obstacles. According to one source:[6]

. . . the Russians got lucky with their new Embassy on Tunlaw Road on one of the highest hills in Washington. When they were assigned the land, private telephone monitoring was unknown and *no one took into account that the site bestrides some important microwave beams.* A primary telephone trunk group for the Eastern seaboard runs close by on the relay between microwave towers in Arlington, Virginia and Gambrills, Maryland. A Defense Department digitized voice circuit from the Pentagon to Western Union's Tenley Tower on Wisconsin Avenue passes almost directly over the [Embassy] site. [Emphasis added]

Another convenience for the Russians is a large long-distance listening device which they have installed in Cuba to monitor U.S. communications satellite messages. The United States, of course, has similar devices to check up on what the Soviets are doing.

Defense against this sort of electronic snooping is very difficult. Bombardment of the accessor by microwave, as practiced by the Soviets against the U.S. Embassy in Moscow, is in most instances impractical. Telephone traffic could be returned to underground cables, and in some instances, with the help of fiber optics, this is being done. But it becomes more and more difficult as traffic increases.

One effective protective measure which can be used for digitized data is to encrypt or code it during transmission. Beyond the problem of foreign espionage, there is a severe problem of ensuring simple privacy of the data on individuals, matters of confidentiality, and the proprietary information contained in these communications. In 1973, as more and more sensitive private information began to be transmitted from computer to computer and the need to safeguard it grew dramatically, the National Bureau of Standards, together with IBM, and with the advice of the National Security Agency, produced a civilian standard cipher called DES (Data Encryption Standard). This is now extensively used by businesses and by U.S. government agencies for unclassified messages.[7]

DES became the instant center of controversy, however, especially since this was a period in American history when nobody trusted anybody. Some people claimed that DES was too weak—even that it had been deliberately weakened to permit the National Security Agency to break the code. These individuals demanded that the key be lengthened. And there were counterarguments that this would be too costly.

The interesting thing that has happened here is that the United States has witnessed the first of doubtlessly many national public debates on cryptology. Public workshops were set up and newspaper articles written for the first time on this ultrasecret subject. Some of the questions which have emerged from these debates have been raised by David Kahn and others:

- What is the proper diplomatic response of a nation to having its communications intercepted by another nation?
- Should a government help its nationals protect their communications from foreign snoopers? Would it be appropriate in a democracy for the Defense Department (NSA) to do so?
- Should it be permissible for private individuals in universities or elsewhere to develop and publish cryptographic techniques? Would this endanger national security? Or do First Amendment rights to freedom of expression take precedence over national security needs?

The sorting out of these and a host of other questions is a part of an evolutionary process made both possible and necessary by the increased capabilities of communications and information technologies.

ONE BILATERAL RELATIONSHIP

Part III

U.S.-Canadian Communications and Information Relationships as a Case Study*

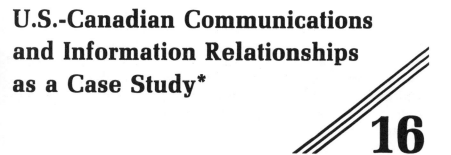

16

CANADA is exceptional in being the first country to recognize the full range of connections among the various communications and information resources. It has also been among the first to see and study extensively the importance of these phenomena to its political and economic processes and to its cultural and legal thinking. It has been among the first to use the newest of these resources specifically to establish strong communications links with its remote areas, and more broadly, to stay in the forefront of the newest technological developments. In fact, it could be said that Canada is highly developed, despite geographic dispersal, *because* of modern communications.

The Canadian government sees communications and infor-

* Condensed from reports by the Program on Information Resources Policy, Harvard University, in 1979 and 1980. Copyright © 1979, 1980 by the President and Fellows of Harvard College. Printed by permission.[1]

mation resources as very important to its economy, and the influx of non-Canadian (mostly American) content in publishing, broadcasting, and film products is seen as a serious threat to a unified sense of Canadian identity. More than any other country, Canada is moving increasingly toward a comprehensive communications and information resources policy to guide its domestic and international affairs. This policy includes a trend in the direction of restrictions on free trade, primarily aimed at its main trading partner, the United States. These potential restrictions take a variety of both overt and covert forms. But, concurrent with these difficulties, the United States and Canada have close and congenial cooperation in many and varied communications and information-related areas.

Canada is a highly developed country, with all of the characteristics and problems of the other OECD nations. On the other hand, its large areas of difficult terrain, the varied needs of its ethnic groups, and the essentially branch nature of its economy make Canada's difficulties in some ways relatable to those which developing countries must face.

Canadian Unity, Economic Viability, and Cultural Identity

The three main political concerns which occupy Canada's leaders are the nation's unity, its economic viability, and its cultural identity, and U.S.-Canadian communications and information relationships were looked at in that context.

The problems surrounding the French-speaking Canadian province of Quebec are quite widely known. But there are other divisive forces with which the Canadian Confederation must contend. The individual Canadian provinces and territories have considerably more power than the states in the United States. The Western and Prairie provinces are attempting for one reason or another to gain greater and greater levels of independence from the Federal Government, and look to Quebec to gain concessions which they can then emulate. The provinces vary widely in their wealth and resources.

Alberta, for instance, has oil, and Ontario is highly industralized, while the Maritime provinces and the Northern territories have difficulties making a living. These various forces, which create unrest and thus threaten Canadian unity, constitute the most critical problem the Canadians must face.

If national unity is Canada's first concern, the economy runs a close second. A growing inflation rate, a slowing of the real GNP, a falling Canadian dollar on the international money market, an increasing trade deficit, and high and rising unemployment all cause great concern. Trade deficits in the manufacturing sector are especially disturbing to Canada, and the constantly increasing deficit in trade in high-technology manufactured goods is even more so. This latter is contrary to trends in the United States, where a favorable balance of trade in high technology has been maintained and increased.

Cultural identity, or a Canadian national identity, is the third major item of Canadian concern. Canada is composed of many separate groups of people who retain their own identities rather than emulating the American melting pot. The lack of a clear-cut, unified Canadian culture on which they can focus means that English-speaking Canadian school children know more about American history and folklore than about the conquering of the Canadian West. This, plus proximity to the United States, also means that the majority of English-speaking Canadians read American books, watch American TV shows, read American magazines, view American films, and enjoy other American entertainment, both through imports and by direct access across the border.

The issues of unity, economic viability and the Canadian search for identity color the Canadian government's perception of the need for a healthy, strong, independent and *Canadian* communications and information policy. Out of its special circumstances, Canadian public policy reflects a much greater awareness than that of the United States of the power exerted by communications and information resources. Unlike the U.S. government, that of Canada looks at these resources in an integrated fashion, and has gone to great lengths to study their role and importance for their country. It sees communications as a major force in bringing about national unity. Canada considers a healthy industry in the communications and information area a high economic priority, and technological sovereignty in this area as essential to the country's future well-being. The development of satellites, of telecommunications, of broadcasting, of publishing industries, of computer communications, and, most especially, of their own research and development are felt to be central to finding answers to their most important problems.

Telecommunications has been a major dynamic force in Canada. The Canadian telephone system is one of the most highly advanced in the world, and just over 96 percent of Canadian households have telephones. Television of all types is available to 96.8 percent of all Canadian households, and radio is available to 98.5 percent. Canada is probably the most "wired" society in the world, with more than 2.7 million cable television subscribers, or 40 percent of its TV viewing market in 1978. In January 1981, about 25 percent of U.S. households with TV had cable.[2]

So close are U.S.-Canadian telecommunications that the two telephone systems are integrated into a single area code system. The telephone system itself is big business between the two countries, with a gross joint message and private line revenue of about $500 million a year. (The figure for U.S.-Mexico, calculated in the same way, is a little less than half—about $225 million.)

Computer Communications

Among the most significant commercial and political stakes for the United States in the computer communications area with Canada are those involving the maintenance of free transborder data flow. The efficiency of the U.S. corporate operations and the protection of U.S. export markets are involved here, as is the principle of free flow of information. More important than the present dollars and cents is that any unfavorable precedent set with a friendly country like Canada could have worldwide implications.

Canada is among the few countries to have attempted to calculate the cost of having data processed in another country, in terms of loss of balance of payments, loss of jobs, and loss of managerial opportunities. But there is a good reason why American businesses want to keep their computer communications services headquartered at home, and why Canadian businesses often want to buy theirs abroad: Canadian tariffs, a 12 percent federal sales tax on equipment, and higher Canadian than U.S. salaries make computer services 20 to 25 percent more expensive in Canada than in the United States. The economies of scale, present in the United States and absent in Canada, also operate to make U.S. services less expensive.

In an effort to retain data processing within Canada, two pieces of legislation were introduced by the Canadian Parliament in 1978. The first was a proposed amendment to the Bank Act, which would prevent banks from processing, storing, or maintaining data regarding corporate and clients records outside Canada. A revised Bank Act was adopted in 1980, but there is some legal controversy on the extent to which the law restricts data processing outside Canada.[3] The other would have amended the Combines Investigation Act, to enable the Canadian government auditors to maintain access to business records regardless of where they were processed or stored. This would have required that multiple descriptions and records be kept on all data transmitted, processed, or stored outside Canada. This is, of course, costly and would have cut down on the competitiveness of U.S. data processing.

Despite negative reports by two Parliamentary Committees regarding these pieces of legislation, an additional official recommendation was made to the Canadian government to consider the feasibility of extending these restrictions to the insurance and loan industries.

While various Canadian government officials have been contemplating restrictive measures to protect Canada, the Canadian computer services industry feels itself capable of competing if left alone or given a few breaks. Canadian industry would like to see the business climate in Canada made less expensive and therefore more competitive. It would like to see the tariffs on computer imports removed, making it cheaper for Canadians to buy U.S. or other foreign-made processing equipment. Some Canadian industry spokesmen decry the Government's omnibus approach to restricting transborder data flow, and think it should concentrate on correcting abuses rather than seeking universal prohibition.

Actual legislation by Canada is not the only threat to unrestricted transborder data flow. Pressure is being put on several U.S. companies by the Canadian government to establish their data processing facilities in Canada or to maintain existing ones there. For the United States, the precedential aspects of this question are crucial, since Canada is so far the only country to discuss the possibility of restrictive measures which it openly admits are economic in nature. Elsewhere, such threats have been carefully veiled under the general heading of privacy.

A problem for both sides is uncertainty over what the future will bring. Businesses are reluctant to make investments when they suspect political or legal roadblocks may be erected. American businesses, especially the smaller ones, are edgy about getting in over their heads, and Canadian businesses are likewise nervous over restrictions that may hamper their trade.

The computer communications area in Canada is a classic instance in which an insufficiently large market, too low an investment in research and development, and prohibitive tariffs and other domestic limitations prevent businesses from being entirely competitive under free market conditions. Canada has a sound technological background for approaching the fast moving events in this area. But Canada is deeply, and probably rightly, concerned that this potential economic and technological revolution will sweep over its country, with innovations introduced by foreign branches or through imports, thereby deepening its dependence on foreign, most especially United States, sources.

Broadcasting, Publishing, and Film Industries

As a result of its perception that Canada is being inundated by American media products, the Canadian government has taken steps to protect Canadian content. These have included the protection of Canadian book authors, measures which some of the best Canadian writers feel protect the mediocre among them.

By far the most important of these steps has been the commonly called Bill C-58, which became effective in 1976, making it impractical for Canadian advertisers to buy space in U.S.-owned publications. That is, Canadians who advertise in U.S. publications or on broadcasts on U.S. stations which are primarily aimed at Canadian audiences cannot deduct such advertising expenses from their income taxes. C-58 was said by the Canadian government to be necessary to divert advertising revenues to Canadian publications, most notably from *Time* and *Reader's Digest* to *MacLean's* news magazine or to Canadian television. In turn, it was said that this would aid Canadians to develop their own cultural content, thereby lessening undesirable influence from the United States.

Despite Canadian government denials, this has been interpreted by Americans as an apparent attempt to force *Time* magazine and *Reader's Digest* out of Canada. *Reader's Digest* conformed to Canadian demands by boosting its Canadian content and by forming a new company which was 75 percent owned by a specially created Canadian foundation. But, while *MacLean's*, which was published monthly, increased to weekly in September 1978, the effort to remove *Time* from the scene has not worked so far. In response to Canadian pressure under C-58, *Time* closed its Canadian bureaus, laid off practically all its employees, dropped the Canadian section, cut its Canadian print run by nearly half, *increased* its price, and *lowered* its advertising rate by 60 percent, based on a lower circulation. As a result, it earned $2.4 million in 1978, about double its profits on the last year before Bill C-58 took effect (1975).

Aside from the failure of C-58 to be effective as a deterrent to U.S. cultural content inflow here, it is doubtful whether this maneuver has done Canada much good economically. In the effort to force Canadian companies to use Canadian magazines to advertise to Canadians, the importation of American magazines with more than a certain percentage of Canadian advertising was prohibited by Canada. According to U.S. publishing sources, the unintended result has been that American trade journals are reluctant to accept Canadian advertising if it will deter the circulation of their journals in Canada. Canadian companies seeking to export goods to the United States have thereby lost a show window and cannot possibly profit by this, they say.

In another problem in the publishing area, Canada's Foreign Investment Review Board has denied all future American investment (including transfers of ownership not involving new investment) in the Canadian publishing industry. The divestiture of several previously American-owned Canadian publishing operations has thereby been forced as American publishers have merged or changed ownership.

Many Canadians, among them the best Canadian authors, recognize that the availability of a large American audience and market has given Canadian writers professional exposure and financial success which they could never otherwise have achieved. Those who espouse this position also contend that exposure to a common cultural market has been an enormous boon for all Canadians. It is said by this group that Canadians have riches not available to any other country in the world by virtue of effortless access to current American publications. This easy access, coupled with their own arrangements with the United Kingdom and French publishers, gives Canada, for minimal cost, a command of thousands of pieces of the latest technological information, research reports, and reports of cultural achievements they could not possibly develop for themselves. One Canadian source, in the context of trans-border data flow, expressed great alarm at the prospect of losing access to the *New York Times* Information Bank.

Canadians are also greatly concerned with the amount of U.S. content on Canadian television. Selling TV programming to Canada is excellent business for the United States, and its receipt is demanded by the Canadian people. The U.S. television industry sold distribution rights worth $50 million a year to Canada in 1978—about 20 percent of all U.S. producers' foreign sales. It is said that all of Canada's production could fill only five or six hours a day on two television channels, assuming two or three major sports events a week reduced the produced drama or news program load. The Canadian government is making a valiant attempt to increase the level of Canadian content on CBC to offset American content. But, like other countries, they have found that home-grown TV programming of the type English-speaking Canadians want is too expensive to make more than a dent in overall needs. Four out of every five hours watched by English-speaking Canadian children, for instance, is programming from American sources.

By licensing cable TV, with essentially unlimited American programming, the Canadian government has more or less conceded that there is little it can do to keep Canadian television Canadian. It is probably this frustration which has lent most fuel to the noisiest and most confusing broadcasting issue between the United States and Canada—the problem of advertising by Canadians on U.S. border television station programs.

As in the publishing area, Bill C-58 was used to make advertising by Canadians on U.S. border stations too expensive to be feasible. As in the publishing area, it was said to serve the same purpose: To divert advertising monies to Canadian businesses for the purpose of building up Canadian content, thereby reducing U.S. content, and providing jobs for Canadian artists, etc. In the context of a total U.S. television advertising revenue of $376 million, the amounts involved—thought to be about $9.7 million annually—are miniscule. However, the U.S. Congress has been led to link the willingness of Canada to enter into serious negotiations aimed at resolving the C-58 issues to any relief for Canada from Section 602 of the U.S. Tax Reform Act of 1976, which limits the income tax deductibility of expenses incurred when attending conventions in foreign countries by American businessmen. Since Canada does a large business in entertaining American conventions, as it was intended to, this has been felt economically. Losses to Canada are estimated to be $100 million annually. In August 1980, President Carter also asked Congress to deny U.S. tax deductions for advertising expenses of American companies buying advertising on Canadian TV, in retaliation for the 1976 Canadian restrictions.[4]

Canada has systematically refused to negotiate on this problem, taking the view that Bill C-58 is a strictly internal matter, bearing on sovereignty. It also seems to be holding out for discussion of this and other communications and information issues as a package. The United States, on the other hand, prefers to handle such issues one by one.

A new trade issue of the television area is now shaping up between the United States and Canada concerning cable television. Canadian cable TV companies are free to enter the U.S. market, and the Canadians had invested a quarter of a billion dollars in U.S. cable systems by 1978. But meanwhile, the Canadian government passed legislation limiting the foreign ownership of Canadian cable systems to 20 percent. And Canadian firms are denied the tax breaks on the advertising money they pay to U.S.-owned media, under the by now familiar C-58 tax bill.

There is also an important land mobile radio broadcasting issue along the U.S.-Canadian border, but this is being handled amicably. The UHF spectrum is allocated by the International Telecommunication Union exclusively for television broadcasting. The growth of U.S. land mobile radio services for a variety of emergency and commercial purposes induced the U.S. Federal Communications Commission (FCC) to propose in 1968 that the United States be permitted to use part of this spectrum for these broadcasts. Since this use might interfere with Canada's needs, the FCC entered into negotiations with the Canadian Department of Communications, and these discussions still continue.

Canada has two basic concerns in this regard: It is afraid of possible interference by land mobile users with existing or future over-air television broadcasts, and it feels it needs to reserve all available UHF frequencies for TV, especially in the Quebec City-Windsor corridor. Pressures for French-language stations can be expected to accelerate. But more important, say the Canadians, their population is predicted to increase 42 percent over the 30-year period from 1971 to 2001, and the character of their labor force will increase leisure-time-activity demands, including the demand for TV services. This indicates a substantial future need for additional television stations and thus a greater number of frequencies, they say.

In 1976, an interim arrangement was made to license U.S. land mobile radio stations within 250 miles of the Canadian border, in which it was agreed that as the U.S. land mobile source drew nearer to the border, its power would be decreased by decreasing maximum antenna heights and wattages. The United States considered the agreed-to restrictions more severe than technically necessary but accepted the arrangement as better than none at all. Meanwhile, Canada agreed to use various procedures to attempt to get a more satisfactory and permanent decision. A new but still tentative agreement was arrived at prior to the WARC '79 Conference. This became possible partly because Canada is also under increasing pressure for mobile radio services for its citizens.

Pending final technical discussions, the two sides agreed to share this frequency band between the two services: the upper part of the band to be used for land mobile services, and the lower part for UHF and TV broadcasting. With improving technologies in TV receivers, and through greater efficiency, it is believed that all Canadian TV requirements can be accommodated in this slightly reduced spectrum.

With the principal points of agreement in place, it appears that an important area of potential disagreement has been eliminated. While further adjustments may be necessary, this issue has been handled in a way which illustrates a constructive give-and-take approach by the agencies of both governments.

Communications Satellites

The United States and Canada have a very satisfactory cooperative relationship in the area of satellites. A number of problems are already present, however, and can be anticipated to increase, as this area expands.

There are presently four rather well-defined communications satellite issues between the U.S. and Canada.

- There is a cultural conflict for Canada in its desire for domestic direct broadcasting satellite transmission (DBS-TV), since this raises the specter of the importation of even more U.S. content.
- There is a matter of who will get the profits—the United States or Canada—and under what conditions, for the types of communications which have until now been handled in a mutually satisfactory way between the Canadian telephone systems (Bell Canada-TCTS) and U.S. Bell, but which in the future may either go to or be affected by satellite transmissions.
- Canada, having launched the third of its Anik series of communications satellites, all made by U.S. prime contractors, is now turning to Canadian prime contractors. But economically, Canada cannot afford to plan beyond a fourth Anik series, and even for Anik D, cannot divorce itself entirely from U.S. technological help.
- Canada, having successfully experimented with the United States on the Hermes (CTS) satellite, now wishes to move to an operational direct-broadcasting system for its nation. But this requires U.S.-Canadian and ITU agreement on a frequency for which the United States and Canada have conflicting needs.

Since the first communications satellite was launched, each successive generation has had greater communications capacity and higher radiative power, meaning that smaller earth stations can be used. This trend may result in direct rooftop-to-satellite-to-rooftop communications in the early 1980s. In early 1979, the Canadian Department of Communications ordered small receiving dishes for experimental direct satellite-to-home broadcasting tests. But cultural difficulties are anticipated for an operational DBS-TV system, since such dishes can be trained on a foreign satellite just as easily as on a Canadian one. Any prohibition of such a practice would be almost impossible to enforce.

This problem already exists in remote northern areas, where Canadian signals are not yet available. Here, technically illegal operators train their dishes on U.S. satellites and distribute the received signals to the local community. Signals from an independent station in Atlanta, Georgia, especially, are picked up and made available to Northern Canadian homes. The Canadian government has refrained from interfering, but the subject is one of controversy in Canada.

Bell Canada and other Canadian telephone companies are alarmed at the possibility of excess capacity on U.S. communications satellites by the early 1980s. The projected new U.S. satellite carriers, they say, could possibly sell lower-cost surplus capacity service into Canada, thereby undercutting the already small Canadian market for long-distance satellite communications. To effectively serve its remote and far northern regions, Canada depends for support on traffic generated from business services in the rest of the country. United States satellite carriers might skim off the cream of Canadian business traffic, the Canadians say.

Bell Canada is also concerned that both international and intra-Canadian traffic could be routed via private earth stations and American satellites. For instance, they say, American-based multinational firms could route all their traffic, both Canada-to-Canada and Canada-to-U.S., via SBS satellites, thereby bypassing Canadian networks completely.[5]

One important goal of Canada's space satellite communications program has been geopolitical, in the sense of a perceived need for occupancy of frequency bands. Canadian planners are afraid that if Canada does not act quickly, the United States will become an early exploiter of these frequency bands and that U.S. mass media penetration into Canada will be even further enhanced.

Canada has not only been swift to occupy synchronous orbits but has constantly attempted to use higher frequency bands for TV broadcasting. The joint U.S.-Canadian cooperation on Hermes (CTS) made Canada and the United States the first nations to experiment with 14/11 GHz frequency bands, for example. With NASA's launching of the Anik B satellite for TELESAT, Canada became the world's first nation to use the higher frequency band for commercial purposes. Canada's concern here is mirrored in developing country desires to have frequencies allocated now for their future use, and to have equatorial parking spaces assigned now for their future satellite needs.

Canada's communications satellite technology has an uncertain future for economic reasons. The Anik D series, due for launch in the early 1980s, will have the Canadian SPAR Aerospace Ltd. as prime construction contractor and U.S. companies as crucial subcontractors. However, TELESAT anticipates no further major procurements of spacecraft until the mid-1980s, for delivery in the late 1980s or early 1990s. Thus, SPAR is entering a field with no long-term expectations. With military programs in the international area generally closed to bidding, Canada's main hope for a viable satellite communications technology industry seems to be through subsystem and consortium bids.

A final problem between the United States and Canada in the communications satellite area deals with Canada's desire to go operational on a domestic DBS system in the next few years. The assignment of frequencies for DBS is regulated through ITU, and Canada cannot proceed without the concurrence of the United States and the ITU, which will meet in Region 2 in 1983.

Communications and Information Factors in the Canadian Economy

Canada's general economy and U.S.-Canadian economic interaction play an important role in U.S.-Canadian communications and information relationships. According to a former Canadian Minister of External Affairs:

> . . . not only is the U.S. our neighbor in a geographic sense . . . it is also the major customer of our products and . . . the most important country in terms of whether our economy will move forward or not. I believe, and indeed the government believes that the maintenance and enhancement of our relations with the U.S. must take a primary priority and is therefore the centerpiece, as it were, of our foreign policy.

June 1979 trade figures attest to the importance to both countries of this economic relationship. In that month, the U.S. took 70.9 percent of Canada's exports and supplied 76.1 percent of Canada's import needs.

The United States, the European Community (EC), and Japan together account for over 80 percent of all Canada's external trade. Of this three-way grouping, more than 60 percent is Canada's trade with the United States. This U.S.-Canadian trade amounted to about $70 billion in 1979—more than U.S. trade with the entire EC. United States direct and indirect investment in Canada is $40 billion—more money than it has invested in any other nation in the world. Great Britain, Canada, and the Netherlands, in that order, have the greatest direct investment in the United States.

The Canadian electronics manufacturing industry comprises 712 firms employing nearly 90,000 people and had total 1975 shipments of $2.59 billion. The average size of these firms is very small by world standards, and only 29 had sales in excess of $25 million a year. The largest, Northern Telecom, employs 19,000 people and has annual sales of nearly $1 billion, but is exceeded in size by at least 30 electronics manufacturing firms in other countries.

Except for Northern Telecom, which is owned and managed by Canadians, the Canadian electronics manufacturing industry is dominated by foreign interests. Of the 100 largest firms, 72 are foreign-owned. Altogether, there are more than 140 foreign-owned firms, accounting for total sales of about $1.4 billion.

The electronics manufacturing industry is the largest industrial employer of technical and scientific manpower in Canada. It is also responsible for about 25 percent of all Canadian industrial spending on research and development. Expenditures on R&D in the electronics industry average between 4 and 5 percent of sales, as compared to about 1 percent for other Canadian industries. Bell Northern Research has the largest industrial research establishment in Canada, employing more than 1400 scientific and technical staff members and spending more than $80 million a year.

Canada's negative trade balance in this sector as a whole had increased to $1.267 billion by 1977, and was believed to be approaching $2 billion in 1978.

It is widely believed in Canada that the manufacture of many kinds of electronic equipment is an impossible task because of foreign competition. But while the manufacture, for instance, of large computers perhaps cannot be supported, that of minicomputers is well within Canada's capabilities. There are other peripheral areas within the computer hardware subsectors which are being successfully exploited by Canadian firms. It is believed that there are opportunities for improvement as well in the subsectors of control and instrumentation, telecommunications, and the category called *other communications.*

In the software field on the other hand, the Canadian performance, already successful in some areas, has an excellent potential. And there is a good domestic market. It is thought that the software market in Alberta alone could be $10 to $20 million per year, and that the total potential market in Canada will be well over $100 million by the 1980s.

Several software firms believe, however, that exports are the key to a "booming" software industry, for to be cost effective in Canada, Canadian-designed packages must be successfully marketed abroad as well as at home. This requires capital investment, and many members of the software industry are critical of the Canadian government's lack of interest in or knowledge of the industry. This is quite ironic in the face of massive Canadian government rhetoric on the importance of communications and information resources!

A significant deficiency in the R&D by the industrial sector of Canada, both as a source of funds and as an R&D performer, has been found. Canadian industry provides only about one-third of R&D expenditures and performs only about 40 percent of R&D, as compared to 40 and 50 percent respectively in other industrialized nations.

The Canadian government realizes the need to support R&D for its high-technology industry, and initiated a modest program of support in 1979. The Canadian government is also trying to "persuade" U.S. businesses operating in Canada to do more R&D there rather than in the U.S. home-based industry. United States business often feels that it can accomplish its R&D more economically or efficiently at home. Business feels that the burden should be on the Canadian government to alter its business climate to make doing R&D in Canada sufficiently attractive both to its domestic and to the foreign-owned businesses.

Besides unhappiness over the level of R&D performed by U.S. subsidiaries in Canada, the Canadian government officials and some nationalists are disturbed about the heavy foreign (U.S.) ownership within the electronics industry. But American business investment strategy in Canada has been historically based on the fact that the Canadian tariff policy encouraged investment. Far from being an unintended side effect of Canadian tariff policy, American investment in Canadian industry has developed out of a conscious and deliberate Canadian objective, with supporters of this high-tariff policy including not just the Canadian government, anxious to promote employment of Canadian workers, but established American subsidiaries as well.

This branch economy problem is *the* problem of the multinational corporation in a generic sense. A branch economy status, however, brings not only problems to Canada, but also the benefits of invisible technology inflows. Such invisible inflows from the United States are estimated to be about $600 to $700 million annually. In 1976, this amounted to $87.5 million in the electronics products field alone, more than matching Canada's $85 million devoted to research in that area.

The Canadian government reacts to this by saying the equivalent of: yes, there are some benefits, but often they do not relate to an exportable product for Canada. And this invisible flow of information leaves Canada vulnerable to foreign decision making and limits Canada's ability to offer adequate employment opportunities to its highly qualified scientists and engineers, technicians and technologists. Most of all, it does not give Canada a chance to stay on top of the very latest technological discoveries and processes. And that is where Canadian industry is hurting most.

COMMUNICATIONS AND INFORMATION RESOURCES IN A GEOPOLITICAL CONTEXT

Part IV

U.S.-Advanced Country Communications and Information Relationships

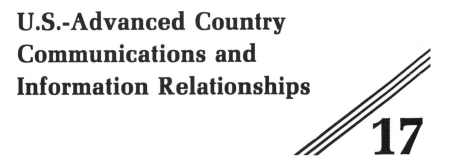

17

THERE are constant interactions between the United States and the other advanced countries which continuously involve the entire spectrum of communications and information resources. For the most part, therefore, these relationships are simply taken for granted. The older communications and information resources have always been the means by which the advanced countries conducted their numerous affairs, and new resources have in general been quite painlessly assimilated.

The United States and other advanced nations are all now entering the information age, and they are entering it at a time of economic, social, and political uncertainty. The heightening energy crisis, the weakening and outmoding of post World War II institutional arrangements such as those resulting from the Bretton Woods Agreement, a changing economic structure, the ever-present threat of Soviet aggression, and the rising expectations of the developing world are challenges which the advanced countries collectively face.

At the same time, the power relationships which have existed since World War II between the United States and the other advanced countries are shifting. The United States is no longer the unchallenged leader of the advanced country allies, but must make accommodations to a number of nations which are growing in economic and technical strength. The Europeans and Canadians see communications and information as a way for the United States to restore its earlier power status in the alliance, and are looking for ways to stop this from happening. In the field of communications and information, the overwhelming lead held by the United States throughout the 1960s and into the 1970s is being diminished as the Western European nations and especially Japan build up their own background industries. This they are more and more determined to do as they come to realize the full significance of the electronics industry—from components to computers to communications to software—for their future well-being. They see the space industries, too, as integral parts of this communications sector, as was made abundantly clear in the French Nora-Minc Report, where communications satellites were included in the term *télématique.*

Faced with heavy dependence on outside energy sources and raw materials in an era of astronomically rising costs, the Japanese are concentrating on the electronics and communications and information industries. And, much more so than the European countries, Japan has been very successful in overcoming its technological gap (which was essentially a management-information gap) of the 1960s with the United States. The Japanese grasp of marketing analysis and techniques, plant acquisition and placement, production scheduling and quality control, and integration of capital information and allocation is gaining them a swiftly accelerating share of portions of the world's communications and information and other markets.

Meanwhile, Western Europe, Canada, and the United States

are suffering from lagging productivity. One way of dealing with this—a way being used by the Japanese—is through improved uses of communications and information especially for automation. This involves the increased use of computers, microcomputers, and robots in production and assembly lines, especially in the steel and automobile industries. This, however, creates other serious dilemmas for advanced countries, since automation and data processing could cause dislocations within industries, or possibly massive layoffs of individual workers. Whether this will actually occur is anybody's guess. Such predictions made in the 1950s and 1960s never were borne out. But the unpredictability of events involved here, at a time of already high and intractable unemployment, has virtually paralyzed the United Kingdom, for instance. This subject is also a source of preoccupation for France, the Scandinavian countries, Italy, and, to a lesser extent, for West Germany. Within the United States, it is not yet a serious question but grumblings indicate that it may very well become so.[1]

But actually, is there any choice? Without updating of plants, techniques, and management, entire industries will fall by the wayside in competition with those who do so update. (The *New Scientist* calls this "the first law of microelectronics."[2])

The collective superiority of communications and information is a very important part of advanced-country defense deterrents to aggression. The NATO allies have highly sophisticated communications and information networks, battlefield equipment, and other armaments based on electronic devices. In the United States alone, $19.2 billion dollars—21 percent of the total defense budget—was projected to be spent for defense electronics in 1980.[3]

Steps are continuously being taken individually through national research and development and collectively through joint research and development, coproduction, and other methods, to keep the alliance well ahead of the Soviet Union in this field. Advanced countries have worked together—sometimes with difficulty—to deny the export of critical technologies to communist countries through an organization called COCOM.* Much of this export control is concerned with communications and information products and technologies because of the possibility of their military use.

The enabling act creating the U.S. National Aeronautics and Space Administration (NASA) called for sharing of space technology internationally. This Congressional mandate has been rather faithfully carried out over the years, with increasing numbers of nations participating in a cooperative manner in space adventures. The nations of Europe, through the European Space Agency (ESA), and Japan are now relatively far advanced in developing their own aerospace industries. Most important, they are attaining their own launch capabilities. This is creating a new balance in international space affairs. For the first time, Europe and Japan now have concrete means for expressing their will and for achieving their own national objectives. As time progresses, this will surely also create new challenges to the integrity of INTELSAT. As they begin to launch their own "domestic" or regional communications satellites, these nations will independently begin to interpret the basic clauses of the INTELSAT Agreement.

New "compunications"† technology is challenging the regulated telecommunications industry in advanced countries. A long-time symbol of sovereignty in Europe—the control of telecommunications by the state-owned PTTs—is being challenged by computing itself. Much of the resentment of Americans and American computer companies by the other advanced nations is bound up in this wider problem. At a time when the United States is moving toward deregulation and toward experimentation with greater competitiveness within the telecommunications industry, most European nations‡ and Japan are not only discouraging competition in telecommunications, but are actively attempting to include computing and

* COCOM is the Coordinating Committee to develop common ground rules for the export of products and technologies to the communist countries. Its membership encompasses all NATO countries, with the loose attachment of Japan.
† Combined computer and communications technology.
‡ The United Kingdom is in some ways an exception.

data processing under the umbrella of their state monopolies. This will cause some severe strains in the coming years in the inevitable trade negotiations regarding communications and information. Such negotiations are already contemplated within GATT and the OECD.

Although the advanced countries may differ on details, they subscribe to the same basic communications and information philosophies.

- They would guard freedom of the press, the free flow of news, and the unencumbered liberty of journalists to collect and disseminate news internationally.
- They are agreed in principle on the necessity for the free flow of data across boundaries.
- Their basic respect for the privacy of individuals is the same.
- All the advanced countries have worked together to develop, and have accepted, the OECD voluntary guidelines on transborder flow of personal data.
- The orderly use of the electromagnetic spectrum is vital to the economic and commercial activities and the national defense of each country. They are agreed that the International Telecommunication Union is an essential institution for achieving this.
- There is general agreement on almost all use of global satellites, although there are important differences, for instance, on direct broadcasting television (DBS-TV).
- The free enterprise system is accepted by all as the most desirable means available for production and commerce, as is the necessity for the dominance of the marketplace to ensure orderly trade in goods and services. This does not carry over to telecommunications, however.
- They are agreed on the need for cooperation on standards, interconnections, and protocols to avoid chaos in international communications. But they are not necessarily agreed on the means for attainment.

The overall future of the developing countries is a concern of the first magnitude for the advanced countries of the world. As foci of political unrest, these countries contain the seeds of violent outbreaks which could lead to a conflict enveloping the world. The enhancement of the well-being of the developing nations is therefore not a choice but a necessity for the advanced nations. Along with the preservation of defenses against the USSR, this is among the most important tasks confronting the United States and its allies over the next two decades. The developing countries constitute the largest and the fastest growing market for the industrialized West and for Japan. They are also the source of many vital raw materials, including the most important of all, oil. The OECD countries, on the other hand, together represent almost the total repository of the advanced communications and information technologies. Their challenge is to find a means for moving these capabilities into the less developed countries without damaging the integrity of those countries and while preserving their own philosophical objectives of free trade, free movement, free press, and free enterprise.

The utmost cooperation by the advanced nations with each other is also needed if the newer communications and information resources are to be used to maximum advantage internationally and their accompanying social, economic, political, legal, and regulatory shocks minimized.

General agreement on common sets of goals and needs puts the advanced countries in a good position to work out their relatively minor differences as these new resources cease to occupy peripheral positions in international debates and become key forces to be reckoned with in overall economic, social, political, and security terms.

U.S.-Communist Country Communications and Information Relationships

18

SINCE the introduction of communism as the political system of the Union of Soviet Socialist Republics after World War I, the United States and the Soviet Union have been active adversaries except for a short interlude when they made common cause during World War II. The animosity between the two countries and systems of government is deeply rooted and has dominated U.S. foreign policy and presidential politics for the past thirty-five years. What the United States does is also of the highest concern to the Soviet Union. And since the United States and the USSR are the only two superpowers, their bilateral relationships are of the greatest worldwide concern and import.

Since World War II, efforts by the United States and its allies to contain communism to relatively confined areas of the world have included the waging of two wars, in Korea and in Vietnam.

The relationships between the United States and the USSR have encompassed important communications and information components aside from those regarding encryption, disarmament, intelligence, and military command and control, which have been discussed in previous chapters. The immediate postwar cutting off of communications to the West by the Soviet Union was recorded for history by Winston Churchill in Fulton, Missouri, on March 5, 1946: "From Stettin in the Baltic to Trieste in the Adriatic an iron curtain has descended across the continent."

Ever since that time, the United States and its allies have attempted to penetrate this "curtain" through shortwave broadcasts to the Soviet people, which the Soviet government has, with exceptions to be noted, systematically jammed. This separation of the West from the East was later reinforced by the building of the Berlin wall. Because of the dangers of a "hot" war in the nuclear age, which "could erase the distinction between the victor and the vanquished," a prolonged cold war has been conducted with propaganda as a major weapon on both sides. The U.S. government has also attempted over the years to convince the USSR that it is to its own advantage to adopt at least a little more openness.

Even as the Soviets were attempting to insulate their people from Western ideas both by reducing the possibility of their receiving Western broadcasts and by severely limiting travel into and out of the country, the USSR, as well as the United States, recognized the danger of the risk of war by miscalculation or accident which could result from the lack of, or by unreliable, communications. The Cuban missile crisis in 1962 showed unequivocally the necessity for direct communications between the two heads of the superpower states. And so, on June 20, 1963, the United States and the USSR signed an agreement to permit the establishment of a Direct Communications Link for use in times of emergency. This is more familiarly known to us as the "hot line."[1]

The original hot line consisted of the most reliable communications systems available at that time between Washington and Moscow, which was a wire telegraph circuit that had to be routed from Washington through London, Copenhagen, Stockholm, and Helsinki to Moscow. This had a backup system of a radiotelegraph circuit which was routed from Washington through Tangiers to Moscow. Because it was meant only for use in extreme emergencies, each system had only one terminal in each country.

By 1971, the hot line had proved its usefulness—in the Arab-Israeli 1967 war, for instance, when it was used to prevent possible misunderstanding of U.S. fleet movements in the Mediterranean. Because it was vulnerable to accidental disruption, bilateral agreement was reached in 1971 to supplement it by one circuit each on the Western INTELSAT and the Soviet Molniya satellite communications systems.

Since its inception, the hot line is publicly known to have been used only sparingly during crisis situations between the two superpowers.[2]

The attempt at detente between the Soviet Union and the United States begun in the early 1970s provided some symptomatic relief to the threat of direct East-West confrontation. But it was not expected to, and did not, change the basic adversary situation. The fact which detractors of the detente effort choose to overlook is that nuclear war is not something that either the U.S. or the USSR can try, and then if the results are unsatisfactory, can go on to bigger and better things. We are, as Henry Kissinger has said, "doomed to coexistence" with the Soviet Union. But it bears remembering that the relationship is not one-sided. The Soviet Union is also doomed to coexist with the United States.

The Soviets know this at least as well as the United States does, and since the death of Stalin in 1953, have made certain attempts to meet the West at least part of the way.

Attempts to communicate with the Soviet Union through the mechanism of scientific, technical, and cultural exchanges were begun by the United States in the 1950s. These were brought to their peak by President Nixon and his Secretary of State, Henry Kissinger. They were continued by the Ford and Carter administrations, but received a serious setback as a result of the Soviet invasion of Afghanistan in 1979.

Multilateral debates between all the Eastern and Western European countries and the United States and Canada over open borders, freedom for jounalists, and freedom of scientific inquiry became the bases for lengthy negotiations known as Basket III of the Conference on Security and Cooperation in Europe (CSCE). This eventually became a part of the so-called Helsinki Agreement of 1975. While the Helsinki Agreement was far from a major breakthrough and did little to improve censorship, freedom of scientific inquiry, freedom to travel outside the Soviet Union, access to sources by journalists, or freedom of political expression for the Soviety citizenry, it did lead to some improvements in communications between East and West. That is, jamming of Western broadcasts ceased, and there was more routine contact with Soviet citizens from the outside world by telephone.* The very fact that the communist world was willing to accept some of the principles of freedom of movement and freedom of expression gives hope and moral support for the eventual improvement of such freedoms.

In the wake of technical and commercial agreements entered into by the governments of the United States and the Soviet Union in 1972 through 1974, scientific and technical exchanges increased, and about 2000 scientists and scientific specialists began to travel across the Soviet border in each direction each year. This led on to visits by several thousand persons with commercial interests and to travel by tourists. While conditions for freedom to travel and to visit facilities in the Soviet Union have been far from perfect and have called for endless exasperating negotiations, this did still represent a major step forward in people-to-people contacts. Formerly, any contact had to have the specific approval of the Soviet Foreign Ministry.

On the part of the U.S. government, the purpose of these

* When the USSR felt its system threatened, by the Polish workers' strikes of August 1980, for instance, it reacted immediately by reverting to jamming.

exchanges was to broaden the base of contacts with Soviet citizens in an effort to lessen tensions, and to create constituencies in the Soviet Union with a stake in maintaining greater contacts with the United States. This effort has in many ways been successful. Trade in technology has expanded a little, but never reached the expectations of either the Soviets or the American business community.

Despite a somewhat better overall understanding between the superpowers during the 1970s, armaments during this period were kept up, and any export of high-technology products or know-how from the United States was scrutinized in detail. Special attention was given to computers, computer components and software, and telecommunications equipment of various kinds, as well as to industrial know-how in these fields. Communications and information items were considered especially sensitive because of their utility in modern intelligence and warfare and because of the U.S. desire to retain its technological lead in this critical area.

Some high-powered computers were exported to the Soviet Union and Eastern Europe, but only after special precautions were taken. These included the careful determination of what use the computer would be put to, and in some instances, provided for the presence of Western technicians to maintain the equipment as well as to conduct safeguard inspections to assure their use for the purpose stated. Spare-part supply was also severely limited so that, should the agreement be violated, the computer would fast be rendered useless.

Although permission to export this type of equipment required an arduous procedure, and the safeguards provided for seemed adequate to many both in government and in industry, there has been major opposition to export of any of this type of equipment or know-how to communist states. Such opposition has been voiced by members of the Defense Department, by the U.S. Congress, and by people from parts of the U.S. electronic industries.

In the aftermath of the Afghanistan invasion, all high-technology goods, services, and data were embargoed for export

U.S. EXPORTS TO THE SOVIET UNION

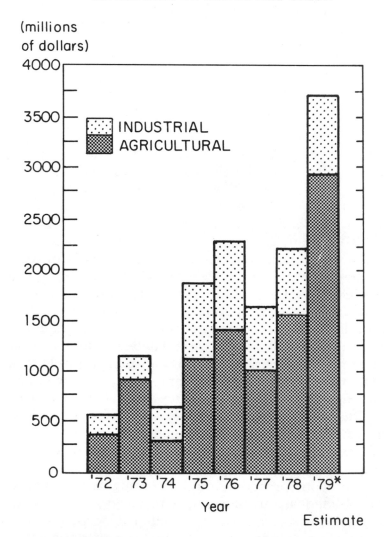

Exports to the Soviet Union are mainly agricultural. Because of their possible use for military purposes, computers and other communications equipment are especially restricted. (From *Newsweek*, January 28, 1980. Reprinted by permission of Leckner Design Associates, Inc.)

to the USSR. Items specifically singled out by the Secretary of Commerce as having "military applications" were digital computing systems and peripheral enhancements for Soviet computers, seismic data processing equipment, research equipment used in the development of microwave and semiconductors, and technical data and equipment for telecommunications plants. Exceptions to the embargo, interestingly, included, for instance:[3] ". . . items whose export serves Western security interests, . . . for servicing needs in connection with safeguards inspections. . . ." Thus, the carefully negotiated safeguard inspections of existing computers and other equipment in the Soviet Union were kept from being jeopardized by this embargo.

Walking the Tightrope and Using the Hot Line

The U.S. government believes that it is three to ten years ahead of the Soviets in computers, miniaturization, and many other electronic techniques and their applications. While the Soviets are capable of producing prototypes of high complexity and utility, it is believed that they experience difficulty in the production of these items in quantity. On the other hand, it is known that the USSR has been able to produce the necessary electronic equipment for intelligence gathering and to run its space program highly successfully. It has a prototype of an antiballistics missile (ABM) system with its attendant communications devices, and a formidable nuclear missile force which could not function without adequate electronic and computer gear.

Despite their basic differences, the United States and the USSR are forced to cooperate on many aspects of communications and information, for their interests are often similar:

- Both nations want to reserve large chunks of the electromagnetic spectrum for military uses.
- Both nations want the freedom to employ "national technical means of verification," and to keep up with each other's military progress.

- Each nation has agreed to forego encryption of telemetry data to permit verification of the other's strategic weapons programs.
- These two pioneers of the space age both have an interest in the orderly evolution of space law.

Because of their opposite ideological views concerning the free flow of information, the United States and the USSR oppose each other in areas of shortwave radio broadcasting, DBS-TV, remote sensing, and the role of the press.

The Soviet Union and the Eastern European countries are not members of INTELSAT but do use the INTELSAT system. Yugoslavia is an INTELSAT member. Algeria recently coordinated the use of INTERSPUTNIK circuits with INTELSAT for public international service. This small step represents no economic challenge to INTELSAT and presents no serious political or national security concerns. But further attempts to extend INTERSPUTNIK to the rest of the world could potentially create serious problems for INTELSAT and have unsettling consequences for Western commercial and government interests. The Soviet Union has recently started to encourage rather aggressively African and other developing countries to join INTERSPUTNIK, and is said to be including earth stations in aid packages.[4]

Scientific and technical agreements also exist with Yugoslavia, Poland, Romania, and the People's Republic of China, through which a certain amount of communications and information technology is exchanged. After the communist takeover in China in 1949, that government lowered a "bamboo curtain" which sometimes made the iron curtain look porous. This effectively cut China off from communications with the outside world until after the death of Mao.

In contrast with its policy with the Soviet Union, the United States is assisting the People's Republic of China with its domestic communications satellites and ground stations. This cooperation began with the Nixon visit to Peking in 1972, with the United States providing both satellite and ground facilities for the dual purpose of keeping a communications lifeline to the United States for the Commander-in-Chief and assuring extensive domestic U.S. television coverage of the presidential visit.

The United States has promised China a communications satellite, but will make delivery in outer space to prevent the transfer of technology. Since the outbreak of hostilities between the Soviet Union and Afghanistan near the Chinese border, China has also been promised a remote sensing ground station and "certain types of early warning radar."

In sum, communications and information relationships between the Soviet Union and other communist nations and the United States are those of an uneasy equilibrium. A communications and information race of astounding proportions has developed between the United States and the USSR, with the former attempting to maintain superiority in the electronic warfare area and the latter attempting to close the gap. Both countries spy electronically on each other for political, economic, technological, and military purposes. The United States attempts to deny communications and information technology and know-how to the USSR, both unilaterally and through its allies. The Soviets, conversely, attempt to obtain it by both overt and covert means.

At the same time, the two nations attempt to create better communications, and to relax tensions generally, to prevent accidental nuclear warfare, and to work toward actual disarmament and keeping of the peace. The hot line which permits direct communications between the President of the United States and the Soviet Head of State thus symbolizes the recognition of each country that the awesome power each possesses must be constantly maintained under the highest level of political control.

U.S.-Developing Country Communications and Information Relationships

19

UNITED STATES and advanced country communications and information relationships are characterized by an abundance of communications and information resources on both sides and generally amiable relations concerning them. United States and communist country relationships are characterized by an equal abundance but a generally negative atmosphere. With the developing countries, these relationships are distinguished by extreme abundance on the U.S. side, extreme scarcity on the other side, and a rapidly rising series of demands for participation in the information age on the part of third world nations.

On an economic basis, the developing countries can be divided into roughly three groups: the so-called "poorest of the poor"; a second group, somewhat better off but still very poor; and a third group, known as the "middle tier" countries, which is on the verge of leaving the developing world and becoming industrialized.

Under theories of aid prior to the mid 1970s, the middle tier countries, which already have the strongest infrastructure, would have been the main recipients of development assistance for the purpose of industrialization. But due to frustrations in the face of intractable problems, changing political attitudes toward aid in the United States, and heavy emphasis on human rights, there has been a shift to the opposite pole. Thus, from the mid 1970s onward, the forty or so poorest countries with the bulk of the 800 million people who live in absolute poverty have become the main recipients of aid, and this aid has been specifically directed toward the poorest of the poor groups within these countries.

"Absolute poverty" has been defined by Robert McNamara, former President of the World Bank, as:[1] "A condition of life so limited by malnutrition, illiteracy, disease, low life expectancy, and high infant mortality as to be beneath any reasonable definition of human decency."

In these countries where people live "on the margin of life" and where national wealth is almost totally absent, there is little room for the provision by the country itself of even the most rudimentary communications systems for governing and for channeling commerce. These countries are, on the whole, politically quiet on the subject of communications and information and their voices are rarely heard in international protest.*

The second, somewhat better off, group of developing nations has passed the stage of abject poverty. These nations have developed civil service systems which at least provide minimal public services, and they enjoy the beginnings of a technical infrastructure and a significant group of educated people. Although they are still battling the most basic problems for many of their citizens, these countries can reasonably plan for a better future and strive toward an active place in the councils of the world.†

* This category includes countries such as Bangladesh, Ethiopia, Mali, Nepal, Zaire, Haiti.

† This category includes countries such as Indonesia, Philippines, Egypt, Ivory Coast, Nigeria, Thailand.

It is this group of countries that most concerns itself with the concept of a New World Economic Order, new rules for world trade and commerce, and with how its image and aspirations are projected in the Western press. Its members are active participants in the debates on the Mass Media Resolution, on satellite orbital space sovereignty, on two-way balanced flow of information, and on redistribution of the world's wealth. These countries are concerned that radio frequencies remain available for their use when they have gained the technical capabilities to benefit from these limited resources. They are the ones who press for prior planning for radio frequencies to guarantee such access.

The middle tier group of developing nations, which are newly industrializing, no longer struggle for their very existence.* But in solving some of the problems of development, they have taken on others. One of these is a massive load of debt. The non-oil-producing states in this category increased their external debt from $142 billion in 1974 to $315 billion in 1978. Sixty-one percent of this was borrowed from private banks.² Advanced-country lenders are not uninterested in the well-being of these countries, for default on these debts could spell disaster for U.S. and other banks and for the world monetary system.

A second problem, which applies to all developing countries but which is especially acute in the middle tier countries, is that they have raised the expectations of their people to a level where failure would bring about severe domestic political and social retribution.

The interests of the middle tier countries lie in greater recognition for their nations, in economic competition on a world basis, in increased industrialization, and in modern agriculture programs. These countries want new rules for world commerce and finance and "a redistribution of the world's labor." They are the most vocal of the developing countries in their demands. They want to protect their infant industries. It is their leaders who strive to upset existing patent and copyright

* This category includes countries such as Brazil, Mexico, Algeria, Taiwan, South Korea, Singapore, Turkey.

conventions, and struggle for binding codes of conduct for multinational corporations and for technology transfer. They advocate a New International Information Order. They agitate for technology and know-how on concessionary terms, for nuclear technology with minimal safeguards, and for advanced military hardware. These are the leaders who, at the 1979 Vienna Conference of the United Nations on Cooperation for Science and Technology for Development (UNCSTD), sought ways to build up the science-based capabilities of the developing world.

The vested interests of the United States in the developing nations are too numerous to mention, but the following are a few examples:

- While the very existence of the United States depends on its relationship with the Soviet Union, the trigger point of disaster is likely to be in the developing world. That volatile unrest exists in these areas is attested to not only by the numerous active post World War II conflicts in countries like Korea, Vietnam, Cambodia, Bangladesh, India, Pakistan, Angola, Uganda, Afghanistan, and so on, but is also reflected in the ways governments are changed.

  According to the *New York Times,* 26 countries, all but two (Spain and Portugal) developing countries, had 46 "unexpected, traumatic or fundamental changes in government" in the decade 1969–1979. Fourteen of these were due to free elections, elections, independence, peace pacts, resignations, or death. But 32, or more than two-thirds, were due to civil war, war, invasion, revolution, assassination or (19) to palace coups or coups.[3]
- The United States wants to minimize communist influence in developing areas. Angola, Somalia, Ethiopia, Yemen, Cuba, and Afghanistan are among the developing countries where communist influence has made inroads.
- The developing countries are major suppliers to and major buyers from the United States. The United States sells more manufactured goods to the developing countries than to the entire European Communities, Eastern Europe, and the Soviet Union combined. Of total U.S. imports, 45 percent comes from the developing nations. This includes not only crucial oil, but also vital minerals and other raw materials. The non-oil-producing developing coun-

tries absorb 38 percent of all U.S. exports and are the fastest growing of all American markets.[4]
- The developing countries outnumber the advanced countries two
  to one and thus have the votes throughout the United Nations
  system to make themselves heard on communications and information and other matters.
- The success of international telecommunications depends upon
  international cooperation. It is necessary to maintain the good
  will of and good working relationships with the developing world
  to ensure progress in this area.
- The United States is deeply interested in maintaining the free
  flow of news across international boundaries, including the boundaries of the developing countries.

In a world of advanced communications, where everyone
sees and is seen on a continuous basis, the differences between
the haves and the have nots have become a constant challenge.
The United States and the other advanced countries can no
longer avoid coming to political grips with this dichotomy.
The other advanced countries have views and interests in
the third world, as expressed through the OECD, the World
Bank, the International Monetary Fund, and other international forums, which are similar to those outlined for the
United States. But while the advanced countries have many
overall common interests in the developing world, their short-
term foreign and defense policy objectives may differ significantly. They also compete there for scarce energy resources
and for markets. All the advanced countries need the economies of scale provided by these markets to overcome the high
development costs of modern communications and information products. Competition for developing country markets
for communications and information equipment, for instance,
promises to be one of *the* future problem areas between the
United States and other advanced countries.

To achieve political stability through development, the advanced nations together must find ways to move their rich
stores of communications and information resources into the
developing world in meaningful and useful terms. But the

transfer of these resources under the best of plans will not be easy. Previous development efforts have amply demonstrated that a resource which works for one country may not work for another. But the advanced countries should not be put off by the theoretical necessity for "appropriate technology," which emphasizes technology that is simple and labor intensive and does not require high capitalization and is therefore usually technology which is behind the times.

Any technology is appropriate that takes root and grows. And the technology that is taking root and growing right now in the developing world is nothing less than the most advanced communications and information technology of all—communications by satellite.

Developing countries now outnumber advanced countries 75 to 30 as signatories of INTELSAT and control one-third of its investment shares, which are based on use.[5] The nature of satellite communications technology, which makes it uniquely capable of reaching into previously inaccessible places, speaks directly to the needs of the developing world. It permits multiple transmission points and the simultaneous use of an unlimited number of earth stations. The system is relatively insensitive to distance, and thus allows low prices essentially without regard to the place where information is transmitted or received. It offers intercontinental telephone, television, data, and computer exchanges, weather and navigational information, and early warnings of disasters. It also promotes the transfer of technology and expertise in telecommunications operations to the developing nations and offers administrative experience in a relevant way.

INTELSAT has made several advantages available to small users who can least afford high capital expenditures. Risks are spread out, equal prices are charged regardless of volume, and a voice is given to small users in the running of INTELSAT. Bulk spare capacity can also be leased for domestic use on a preemptible basis* for about half the usual price. Algeria

---

* This service is subject to interruption for higher priority use, which thus far has not created a problem.

was the first country to use this leased capacity to provide a domestic communications system to its desert population. This developing country has now been joined by sixteen others with domestic systems based on spare INTELSAT capacity. There are plans by INTELSAT to build up non-preemptible capacity specifically for such domestic uses. Another benefit for small users is the SPADE* system, which permits the less costly use of capacity on an as-needed basis. The bulk of traffic on SPADE is between the developing and the developed world.

The INTELSAT Agreement was a farsighted institutional arrangement that permitted nations of differing economic and technological strengths to participate as partners for their mutual benefit. While satellites or other forms of communications are obviously not the panacea for all developing world problems, the INTELSAT success story does demonstrate that advanced communications and information resources offer unique ways to leapfrog over some old and intractable obstacles.

* Single Channel Per Carrier Pulse-Code Modulation-Accesses-Demand-Assigned Equipment (SCPC/SPADE).

EIGHTEEN POINTS FOR FORMULATING POLICY

Part V

The International Policy Environment of Communications and Information Resources

20

ALTHOUGH it has been necessary in this book to single out the communications and information resources sector from others to understand its changing dynamics, this sector cannot and must not be treated in isolation. Communications and information activities are integral parts of and both conform to and influence U.S. domestic and international affairs. The general and then the more specific implications of communications and information for U.S. policy therefore need to be examined.

A prime concern of the United States is to maintain the military and economic security of its own nation and that of the free world. Communications and information must therefore work in harness with this objective, and with policies directed toward this end. The United States wants to maintain the free flow of information and free access to news by correspondents and the news media. It also has a major interest in the use of communications and information technologies for the promotion of development, where the potential is great but almost entirely unexploited, if even understood. The United States is interested in seeing the relatively unencumbered evolution of new technologies. High on the list, and not incompatible with all these interests, is the aid and protection of U.S. business and U.S. markets.

U.S. policy in communications and information will be influenced by patterns set by the policy, institutions, and practices in political, trade, and economic areas; in the technology area; in defense and intelligence; in the area of development; and in·relations with the communist world.

Key Elements of U.S. Policy

Some key elements which dominate U.S. government and private thinking in the areas affecting communications and information policy may be broken down into areas called political, economic and trade, technology, defense and intelligence, and development.

1. *Political.* The United States wants to have continuing good relations with its historical allies and trading partners, and to have friendly, cooperative relationships with as many countries as possible. It wants strong, independent allies, with their own healthy social and economic fabrics. In the developing world, the United States seeks humanitarian goals. It wants to moderate the flames of passion incited by poverty, frustration, overpopulation, urban congestion, and widespread unemployment, both for compassionate reasons and because suffering leads to a propensity to seek relief by going to war. And the United States, of course, wants to maintain access to vital raw materials, and to worldwide markets for U.S. products and services.

2. *Economic and Trade.* The United States wants to improve its balance of payments and balance of trade positions, to stabilize the dollar, and to reduce inflation. Americans are becoming more export-minded, and more conscious of the competitiveness of U.S. products and services in the markets of the

world. Exports grew from 6 percent to 11 percent of total output of U.S. goods and services in the decade 1970–80.[1] The degree of support or hindrance by the government for international trade is a subject of intense debate. Threats of foreign competition or loss of jobs are also active domestic issues.

Basic to all these questions is whether, in fact, the U.S. economy is still manageable essentially in domestic terms. The U.S. economy has become so intertwined with and dependent upon world resources and the international monetary system that, for better or for worse, it operates as a part of the total global system. The implications of this are enormous and have not yet been faced squarely.

3. *Technology.* United States international technology policy, to the extent that it exists, first of all must support U.S. political, economic, and trade policies and its defense objectives. The improvement of innovation and productivity of the domestic economy is a major goal. Throughout the post-World War II era, the United States has freely exported its technology both to OECD countries and to developing nations. This is easy to see, since U.S.-developed technology is available abroad within a very short span of time from its creation. United States aid policies since the days of Truman's Point Four have sought to assist the developing countries in their search for technical answers to their problems. That this has been only partially successful is as much due to the fact that the problems constantly outspace the solutions as it is to any intrinsic failure. The United States tries to assist these nations in building up their infrastructures, in making better choices of foreign technology purchases, and in developing their potential to adapt acquired technology. All this is directed toward the eventual end of creating indigenous technologies.

In space exploitation, which is so important to communications and information, the United States has by legislation consciously sought the cooperation of foreign nationals and nations. Launching facilities have been available to the noncommunist world at cost and without discrimination.

With few exceptions, the United States has favored free

trade in technology. Major exceptions have been made in trade with communist countries on national security grounds, and, under close Congressional scrutiny, occasionally for foreign policy reasons. This includes the embargo to Rhodesia and restrictions on computer shipments to police services of South Africa. The 1979 Export Administration Act, an updated version of U.S. policy for the past two decades, emphasizes the importance of export trade and seeks to minimize restrictions. At the same time, it puts more restrictions than previously on technology and know-how while putting fewer restrictions on finished products. This policy is in line with the recommendations of the Defense Technology Advisory Board Report (the Bucy Report.)[2]

In addition to the above act, the Munitions Control Act directly controls military-related goods and technologies, and matters related to atomic energy are regulated through a number of special laws, including the Nuclear Nonproliferation Act dealing with nuclear security and nonproliferation.

The question of the extent to which export controls in high technology can be used for leverage to influence Soviet behavior on important issues has concerned the United States since World War II, and again reached headline proportions in connection with U.S. reactions to Soviet invasion of Afghanistan. In 1979, computer-related sales accounted for slightly more than 3 percent of total U.S. trade with the Soviet Union, totaling about $25 million—a drop in the bucket. For at least the past decade, the Soviet Union, in any case, has not been confined to U.S. exports, but can obtain very similar technologies from other OECD nations. In the military field, although lagging in certain electronics areas, the Soviet Union is not without its own resources.

4. *Defense and Intelligence.* Deterrence and parity in strategic weapons with the USSR is a primary U.S. defense goal. The cornerstone of this policy is a strong U.S. defense posture, a strong NATO, and a viable Command, Control, Communications, and Intelligence (C^3I) system. Parity or superiority in weapons and communications systems means the outlay of billions of dollars for research and development, for testing

and evaluation, and for the procurement of new products. Modern weapons systems are heavily dependent on all sorts of electronics. This, together with the space effort, has been of major benefit to the building of the civilian compunications sector in the United States.

Intelligence is vital for early warning and for detection, monitoring, and verification of adversary military activities. Forward telemetry bases on land, at sea, and in the air are vital links in the worldwide defense efforts of at least the super-powers. New vulnerabilities of communications and intelligence systems to ordinary enemies, to satellite warfare capabilities, to jamming, and to sabotage by terrorist groups are all new defense worries.

5. *Development.* Congressional disenchantment with aid efforts except humanitarian ones, and the disappointment of the Carter Administration with the results of post-World War II aid policies led it to launch a Basic Human Needs strategy confined to the poorest people in the poorest countries of the world. This strategy was set up as a part of its larger Human Rights policy. Assistance was funneled directly to the poor, or used for their *specific and visible* needs. During the Carter Administration, aid was, therefore, essentially limited to food, health aids (including family planning), and rural development. Industrialization or technical infrastructure building or aid to nations nearing industrialization was specifically excluded. While this approach may benefit the most needy and rural families more directly than did the old "trickle down" policy of stimulating the whole economy, the results are not yet in.

"Basic human needs," as well as "appropriate technologies," are concepts thoroughly mistrusted in the developing world. Third world leaders believe this to be a plot to keep them backward in perpetuity. They believe it to be inconsistent with their aims toward the New International Economic Order, a program designed to assure greater real resource transfer from the developed to the developing world. It was and is a quest for a change in the rules of world trade, the monetary system, and the means of economic efficiency. Under whatever flag or name it will be fought, some type of New International Economic Order concept will be central to economic and political conflict between the world's rich and the world's poor nations for the decades to come.

Why Communications and Information Resources Deserve Policy Attention

The following are eighteen reasons why communications and information resources issues deserve the careful and continuing attention of U.S. private and government leaders and policymakers:

1. The combined communications and information sector market in the United States was roughly estimated to be about $150 billion in 1979. Various astronomical figures are given for its worldwide value by the end of the 1980s. We can rest assured that it will be a lot. The communications and information sector is accounting for larger and larger chunks of the U.S. economy, and it can be safely assumed that this trend will spread worldwide. Within the United States, 50 percent of the labor force already worked in communications and information-related activities in 1970, and the percent of GNP from this sector at that time was at least 30 percent. This, too, is the trend throughout the industrialized world. The communications and information sector is active, dynamic, and growth-oriented, in the presence of general industrial malaise. The top three U.S. industries in total productivity are said to be telecommunications, electric and electronic equipment, and semiconductors. And this group ranks fourth best in U.S. foreign trade, exceeded only by agriculture, arms, and civilian aircraft. Computers and computer-related equipment alone accounted for a positive balance of trade of more than $4 billion in 1979.[3] But to take full advantage of new communications and information devices in the workplace could lead to major conflicts between management and labor in the coming decade.

2. Governments of other countries resent their inundation

U.S. TRADE IN COMPUTERS AND RELATED EQUIPMENT

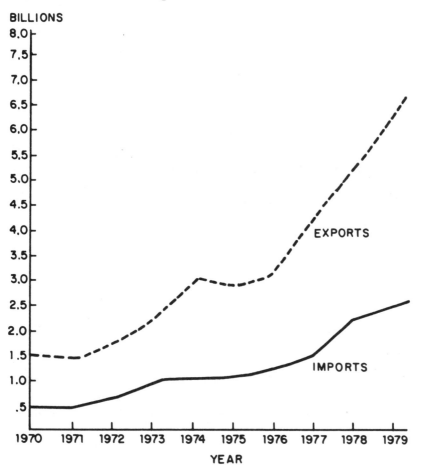

Computers and related equipment rank fourth best as U.S. trade items. They are exceeded only by agricultural goods, arms, and civilian aircraft. (Reprinted by permission of Computer and Business Equipment Manufacturers Association.)

by American information in the form of television programming, magazine, books, newspapers, films, records, and advertising, even as they buy U.S. media products because they like them and because they are cheap. At the same time, they fear being dependent on the United States in what they consider to be a vital new area, communications and information resources. This is especially true of the electronics-based technologies. This combination is leading them to consider various kinds of restrictions on information and its products which cross their borders.

3. Potent ideas such as national sovereignty and cultural identity expressed by some advanced and most developing nations may seem vague and nonspecific. But they express in political terms the fears of the effects of new developments in the communications and information area, and especially of the relentless exposure to alien values these developments bring with them, which could distort the social and cultural fabric of individual societies.

4. The U.S. government and U.S. commercial enterprises must have international communications, whether in the form of voice, data, or facsimile. So must the governments and commercial enterprises of the rest of the world. Perhaps the most obvious examples are international airlines and banks, which cannot exist without international communications and information systems of great complexity.

5. Today's money markets operate twenty-four hours a day, and this has profound effects on market dynamics. It reduces national decision-making control over national currencies, and perhaps undermines a fundamental tenet of national sovereignty.

6. The intelligence services of the superpowers depend on satellites for reconnaisance, for national means of verification of each other's strategic capabilities, and for other functions. This practice has now been recognized and written into international treaties. It has also been recognized that telemetry and other electronic listening posts (bases) on foreign soil, and undersea electronic surveillance devices on the high seas, are essential to modern security needs.

7. The U.S. defense establishment and U.S. diplomatic missions depend on reliable, secure, and rapid international communications for command and control, vital decision making, and for the execution of orders of the most critical nature for national survival.

8. The availability of microelectronic components makes possible the production of critical defense hardware, and the scarcity of these same components as surely prevents it. Provision or denial, and dependability of access, are therefore international issues.

9. The United States is being challenged in a number of communications and information areas by other nations who are catching up in the electronics and computer areas and are thus threatening U.S. post-World War II technological leadership. The capability of France and Japan of launching their own satellites has changed the status quo and has added new dimensions to the functioning of INTELSAT and other outer space activities.

10. Communications and information technologies are among the most sensitive of all technologies to be singled out by the U.S. government for strategic and foreign policy export control reasons.

11. International, as well as domestic, communications/computer networks are increasingly vulnerable to interference by unfriendly nations and by terrorist groups, and to eavesdropping. They are also susceptible to simple breakdown. With growing dependence on these systems, vulnerability is increasing proportionately.

12. The news media, and especially television, rely more and more heavily on real time broadcasts from points of interest and trouble spots globally. Satellite transmission, videotape, and portable electronic cameras permit news coverage from almost any part of the globe. While this makes for greater worldwide awareness, it also contributes to international tension.

13. The principle of free flow of information, the cornerstone of U.S. information policy since World War II, is being challenged by developing nations. Newsmen have increasing

difficulty in gaining access to news, and must take more personal risks to achieve success. Developing countries are demanding a New International Information Order, viewing know-how as information, and insisting upon access to technological know-how on concessionary terms. Information is in all ways fast becoming more valuable as a commodity on world markets.

14. With rapid and extensive data flow across international boundaries, and the use of readily accessible and retrievable computer data files, threats to privacy of personal data have become an international issue.

15. The right to broadcast, via shortwave or TV, without prior consent of the recipient nation—or conversely, the right to protect national integrity by jamming, for instance—is a subject of debate between the U.S. and communist countries, the U.S and the less developed countries, and the U.S. and Canada.

16. The electromagnetic spectrum needed for broadcasting, data transmission, scientific uses, remote sensing, and a variety of other purposes is limited. Its allocation is therefore the subject of increasing competition and dissension among nations.

17. Almost by definition, communications and information is not confined within national borders, and almost by definition, the information society will be built by a series of events affecting many nations simultaneously. The question then is: Can and do multinational organizations, as now set up to handle specific categories of problems, meet the needs for the multilateral resolution of communications and information disputes? Profound changes in global societies may also be surpassing international legal arrangements. New or revised ones will be debated in the coming decade. The United States faces important decisions here, especially in determining whether a comprehensive law regarding international communications and information will be required.

18. Nearly twenty major policy level international conferences on matters related to communications and information

questions are already scheduled to be held within the next five years. The outcome of each has potentially important ramifications for U.S. business, the U.S. economy and security, and for U.S. news-gathering and distribution activities.

Summary

This book has pointed out the all-pervasiveness, variety, and interdependence of the swiftly accelerating communications and information resources and their importance to U.S. business strategy and governmental policy. The international implications of communications and information resources have been shown to be far-reaching. A new framework for understanding both the domestic and the international spheres of communications and information would seem to be indicated. Separation of problems into neat compartments, such as domestic vs. international, economic vs. political, transmission vs. content, civilian vs. military, strategic vs. civilian trade, domestic vs. multinational corporations vs. foreign firms, national security vs. civil liberties, government-conducted foreign policy vs. media diplomacy, military vs. economic intelligence, and privacy vs. freedom of information, no longer has relevance. Nor can categorization by upcoming international conferences or by topic problems, such as WARC, the Mass Media Resolution, international civil encryption, national means of verification, support to military operations, or computer/communications, enlighten the U.S. policymaker in industry or in government.

Increasingly, all these matters are uncomfortably merging because of the evolving technologies; the shrinkage of the world through communications; the changing defense and intelligence needs in the nuclear age and the age of terrorism; the growing economic, monetary, and political interdependence of nations; and the wholesale democratization of peoples through radio, television, telephone, and the tape recorder and cassette.

The changes which communications and information resources have brought about are of such potential importance and may affect so deeply the way the world lives, works, and organizes its societies that it is important for the United States to ask itself some broad questions about what it really stands for and what it really wants. For, as the Canadian Deputy Minister of Communications has said:

It is important that those who make or influence policy return to basic principles, when confronted by changing realities . . . not since the industrial revolution have we seen such dramatic changes in the structure of our economies. In the industrial era, many laboured, and information was the tool of the elite, the instrument of management or of government. Information was a scarce commodity. Information was power. Today we have seen information percolate down through the echelons of society to an ever-increasing extent. . . . And as it reaches ever further down . . . information is being transformed from power to wealth. We have entered a new age, a new economy, whose rules are as yet undefined, whose realities are as yet undetermined.

The challenge for America is to help guide these realities in fruitful directions and, by conscious deliberation, assure that the press of events will not determine the ground rules.

APPENDIX

Notes

1 The Challenge to America

1.1 J. J. Servan-Schreiber, *The American Challenge*, Atheneum, New York, N.Y., 1968.

1.2 John W. Kendrick, *Impacts of Rapid Technological Change in the U.S. Business Economy and in the Communications, Electronic Equipment and Semiconductor Industry Groups*, paper presented before the OECD Working Party on Information Computers and Communications Policy, Paris, November 27–29, 1979; Charles P. Lecht, *The Waves of Change: A Techno-Economic Analysis of the Data Processing Industry*, Advanced Computer Techniques Corporation, New York, N.Y., 1977; Edward W. Scott, "Multifunction Application at a Medium/Large Site," *Automated Business Communications*, International Data Corporation, Waltham, Mass., 1979; Merrill Sheils et al., "And Man Created the Chip," *Newsweek*, June 30, 1980, pp. 50–56.

1.3 Peter J. Schuyten, "Semiconductor Buyer Fever," *New York Times*, October 11, 1979.

1.4 Hobart Rowen, "Blumenthal Talks About What 'Went Wrong' in Policy," *Boston Globe*, October 31, 1979.

1.5 Pierre Juneau, Deputy Minister, Department of Communications, Canada, *National Information in the Global Environment*, an address to the Workshop on Strategic Implications of the Changing Telecommunications Environment of Newspapers, Harvard University, Program on Information Resources Policy, November 11, 1980.

1.6 André Giraud, Minister of Industry, France, opening address to the High Level Conference of the OECD on Information, Computer and Communications Policy in the 1980s, Paris, October 6, 1980.

2 From Scarcity to Abundance

2.1 John W. Kendrick, *supra* note 1.2; Bill Laberis, "Labor Stats: DP Industry to Skyrocket in '80s," *Computerworld,* October 12, 1981, p. 29; "The Front-Runners in a Restructured Economy," *Business Week,* June 1, 1981, pp. 94–98.

2.2 Anthony G. Oettinger, personal communications.

2.3 Charles P. Lecht, *supra* note 1.2.

2.4 Ibid.; Edward W. Scott, *supra* note 1.2; Peter J. Schuyten, "A Desktop Computer by I.B.M.: Giants Converge on Tiny Market," *New York Times,* February 6, 1980.

2.5 "The Uneven Impact of Price Increases," *Business Week,* February 11, 1980, p. 32; Charles P. Lecht, *supra* note 1.2.

2.6 Oswald H. Ganley, *Transborder Data Flow—A Significant Factor in World Trade?,* paper presented at conference on Transnational Data Flows, Washington, D.C., 1979.

2.7 John Bardeen, Walter H. Brattain, and William Shockley shared the 1956 Nobel Prize for physics.

2.8 Oswald H. Ganley, *supra* note 2.6.

2.9 Edgar A. Grabhorn and Alan B. Kamman, "Size and Potential of the World's Telecommunication Markets," *Inteltrade,* Vol. 3, No. 1, January 15, 1980, pp. 8–9.

2.10 "The Opec Decade," *The Economist,* December 29, 1979, p. 53 ff.

2.11 Robert Cooke, "New Technology Will Put a Twinkle in Ma Bell's Voice," *Boston Globe,* January 24, 1980.

2.12 Irving Goldstein, *What Next for International Satellite Communications: Issues and Problems for the 1980s,* Harvard University, Program on Information Resources Policy Seminar, October 6, 1980.

2.13   Stephen E. Doyle, lecture presented at the John F. Kennedy School of Government, Harvard University, Fall 1979.
2.14   Ibid.

3   Dynamics within the U.S. Communications and Information Resources Sector

3.1   John F. McLaughlin and Anne E. Birinyi, *Mapping the Information Business,* Program on Information Resources Policy, Harvard University, Cambridge, Publication P-80-5, July 1980; Benjamin M. Compaine, *A New Framework for the Media Arena: Content, Process and Format,* Program on Information Resources Policy, Harvard University, Cambridge, 1980.
3.2   John F. McLaughlin and Anne E. Birinyi, *supra* note 3.1.
3.3   Anthony G. Oettinger, "Information Resources: Knowledge and Power in the 21st Century," *Science,* Vol. 209, July 4, 1980, pp. 191–198. "The digital technologies underlying such devices are a merger of computer and communications technologies into a common stream that I have called compunications technologies" (p. 191); Simon Nora and Alain Minc, *The Computerization of Society: A Report to the President of France,* MIT Press, Cambridge, 1980.
3.4   William H. Read, *The First Amendment Meets the Second Revolution,* Program on Information Resources Policy, Harvard University, Cambridge, Publication P-81-1, 1981.
3.5   John F. McLaughlin and Anne E. Birinyi, *supra* note 3.1.
3.6   *Second Computer Inquiry,* FCC Docket 20828, *Final Decision,* released May 2, 1980, 77 FCC 2d 384 (1980), Order No. FCC 80–189; *Computer Inquiry,* FCC Docket 16979, *Final Decision and Order,* released March 18, 1971, 28 FCC 2d 267 (1971), Order No. FCC 71–255.
3.7   Desmond Smith, "What Is America's Secret Weapon in the Energy Crisis? Your Television Set," *Panorama,* April 1980, pp. 28–33.
3.8   "Exxon's Next Prey: IBM and Xerox," *Business Week,* April 28, 1980, pp. 92–103.

4   Communications and Information Dynamics within General U.S. Industry

4.1   U.S. Department of Commerce, Office of Telecommunications, *The Information Economy: Definition and Measurement,* by

Marc Uri Porat, OT Special Publication 77–12 (1), Government Printing Office, Washington, D.C., 1977.

4.2 Based on several sources, including McCaffery, Seligman & von Simson, Inc., *Impact of Transborder Data Flow Legislation,* Vol. II: *Corporate Case Studies,* October 1979; personal communications.

4.3 Based on several sources, including James Harding's lectures at the Kennedy School of Government, Harvard University, 1979, 1980.

4.4 "A Bigger Load for Rail Computers," *Business Week,* February 4, 1980, pp. 89–90.

4.5 M. H. Crawford, *Microelectronics and Telecommunications in the Workplace,* unpublished draft of paper presented before OECD Working Party on ICCP Special Session on the Impact of Microelectronics on Productivity and Employment, Paris, November 27–29, 1979 (DSTI/ICCP/79.62/07).

4.6 "Ford Saves $180M with Transnational Design Net," *Transnational Data Report,* Vol. 3, No. 6, October 1980.

4.7 Oswald H. Ganley, *supra* note 2.6.

4.8 Ibid.; "Visa Reports Decline in Profitability, Citing Costs and Credit Curb," *Wall Street Journal,* May 9, 1980.

4.9 "Saved by (Ma) Bell?" *Advertising Age,* April 7, 1980.

4.10 McCaffery, Seligman & von Simson, Inc., *supra* note 4.2.

5 The World Picks Up the Economic Challenge

5.1 U.S. Department of Commerce, Office of Producer Goods, *A Report on the U.S. Semiconductor Industry,* Government Printing Office, Washington, D.C., September 1979.

5.2 Bohdan Szuprowicz, "South Africa is Attracting Electronics Manufacturers," *Computer Data,* Vol. 5, No. 1, January 1980.

5.3 Japan Information Processing Development Center, *Computer White Paper,* 1977 ed.

5.4 Simon Nora and Alain Minc, *supra* note 3.3.

5.5 Ibid.

5.6 Charles P. Lecht, "Tsunami," *Computerworld,* November 1978–January 1980 (appeared intermittently).

5.7 Ibid.

5.8 Richard Veith, "National Planning, Computers and Informatics," unpublished paper PPA/POS 708, April 1979.

5.9 Simon Nora and Alain Minc, *supra* note 3.3.

5.10 Canada, Consultative Committee on the Implications of Telecommunications for Canadian Sovereignty, *Telecommunications and Canada* (Clyne Report), Ottawa, 1979.

5.11 Commission of the European Economic Communities, *European Society Faced with the Challenge of New Information Technologies: A Community Response (Davignon Report)*, Brussels, November 26, 1979.

5.12 Amy Newmark, "Telecommunications in Brazil," *Inteltrade*, Vol. 1, No. 11, October 30, 1978, pp. 2–6.

5.13 U.S. Congress, House Committee on Ways and Means, Subcommittee on Trade, *High Technology and Japanese Industrial Policy: A Strategy for U.S. Policy-makers*, WMCP: 96–74, 96th Cong., 2d Sess., October 1, 1980; "Japan's Chipmakers Start the March on Europe," *The Economist*, January 26, 1980; "The Robot Revolution," *Time*, December 8, 1980; Justin Bloom, personal communications.

5.14 Based on several articles, among them: Paul Lewis, "Europe Joins Microchip World: Competition Heats Up with U.S. and Japan," *New York Times*, January 29, 1980.

5.15 Morris Crawford, personal communications.

5.16 Harvey Brooks, personal communications.

6 Regulatory Activities in Communications and Information Competition

6.1 Vico E. Henriques, "Telecommunications and Foreign Trade: The Dominant Issues of the '80s," *Computerworld*, December/January 1979, p. 59; Morris Crawford, personal communications.

6.2 George Curuby, *The Regulation of the Information Industries in Europe—The Growing Communications Gap*, unpublished paper, Harvard University, Fall 1979.

6.3 Stephen Banker, "For Cable TV, It's a One-Way Border," *TV Guide*, January 12, 1980, pp. 31–36.

6.4 Adrian R. D. Norman, "Compatibility, Harmonisation and Interworking—The Future of Open International Systems," *Communications, Information Processing, and Productivity Revolution*, ADL Consultants Report at the Third Annual Arthur D. Little Executive Forum in International Telecommunications, Innisbrook, Tarpon Springs, Florida, November 7–9, 1979; "Tying National Telecommunications into an International Network," an interview with Richard E. Butler, Deputy Secretary-General of the International Telecommunication Union, *Inteltrade*, September 30, 1979, pp. 7–12.

7   The Changing Role of the Media in International Affairs

7.1   Larry S. Levine, *Television Program Exports*, report prepared for Research Program on Communications Policy, MIT, Cambridge, 1980.

7.2   Jack Valenti, Statement before U.S. Congress, Senate Committee on Foreign Relations, International Communications and Information, Hearings before the Subcommittee on International Operations, 95th Cong., 1st Sess., June 8, 9, and 10, 1977, p. 209.

7.3   William H. Read, *America's Mass Media Merchants*, Johns Hopkins University Press, Baltimore, 1976.

7.4   Ibid.

7.5   Rosemary Righter, *Whose News? Politics, the Press and the Third World*, Times Books, New York, N.Y., 1978.

7.6   Oswald H. Ganley, *The Role of Communications and Information Resources in Canada*, Program on Information Resources Policy, Harvard University, Cambridge, Publication P-79-1, June 1979.

7.7   Paul Hannon, "U.S. Films Enjoy an Export Boom," *Boston Globe*, September 11, 1980.

7.8   Andrew Heiskell, *Communications: Some Full-Grown Progeny of a Recent Marriage*, remarks by the Chairman of Time Incorporated at The Economic Club of Detroit, March 10, 1980.

7.9   Michael Mosettig and Henry Griggs, Jr., "TV at the Front," *Foreign Policy*, No. 38, Spring 1980, pp. 67–79.

7.10   Edward Planer, *The Impact of Technology on Television News*, lecture, John F. Kennedy School of Government, Harvard University, Fall 1979.

7.11   CBS, "Evening News," January 27, 1981, Commentary by Eric Sevareid.

7.12   Jonathan Gunter, *The United States and the Debate on the World "Information Order,"* Academy of Educational Development, Washington, D.C., August 1978.

7.13   Michael Mosettig and Henry Griggs, Jr., *supra* note 7.9

8   "Free Flow Forever" vs. "Objective and Balanced News"

8.1   From an address by Mr. Amadou-Mahtar M'Bow, Director-General of UNESCO, at the closing of the Intergovernmental Conference for Co-operation on Activities, Needs and Programmes for Communication Development, Paris, April 21, 1980.

8.2   International Commission for the Study of Communication Problems, *Interim Report on Communication Problems in Modern Society,* UNESCO, CC-CIC-78/WS/39, Paris, September 1978, p. 78.

8.3   Leonard Marks, "A Global Communications Order," in *Issues in Communications,* No. 2, 1978, International Institute of Communications, London, p. 8.

8.4   Ibid.

8.5   Ibid.

8.6   Archibald Cox, "The Supreme Court 1979 Term: Foreword: Freedom of Expression in the Burger Court," *Harvard Law Review,* Vol. 94, No. 1, November 1980, pp. 1–73.

8.7   U.S. Congress, Senate Committee on Foreign Relations, and House Committee on Foreign Affairs, *Reports Submitted to Congress Pursuant to the Foreign Relations Authorization Act, Fiscal Year 1979 (Public Law 95–426),* Joint Committee Print, 96th Cong., 1st Sess., Washington, D.C.: Government Printing Office, 1979, p. 100.

8.8   *Final Act of the Conference on Security and Co-operation in Europe* (Helsinki Declaration), 1975.

8.9   International Commission for the Study of Communication Problems, *supra* note 8.2.

8.10   "The Media and the Goats" (editorial), *New York Times,* November 27, 1978.

8.11   International Commission for the Study of Communication Problems, *Final Report (MacBride Reports),* Part Five: *Communication Tomorrow,* Paris, 1980.

8.12   Jonathan Gunter, *supra* note 7.12 at p. 60.

8.13   John E. Reinhardt, *Towards an Acceptable Concept of the New World Information Order,* an address before the US-Japan Symposium, Fletcher School of Diplomacy, Tufts University, Medford, Mass., October 11, 1979; John E. Reinhardt, *The Free Flow of Information: Problems and Prospects,* seminar at the Program on Information Resources Policy, Harvard University, Cambridge, April 2, 1979.

9 Transborder Data Flow (TBDF) Restrictions

9.1 Richard Veith, *supra* note 5.8.

9.2 William Pitt the Elder, quoted in American Bar Association, *Preliminary Proposal to National Science Foundation for Symposium on Personal Privacy and Information Technology*, Chicago, 1979, p. 1.

9.3 Louis Harris & Associates, Inc., and Alan F. Westin, *The Dimensions of Privacy: A National Opinion Research Survey of Attitudes Toward Privacy*, Sentry Insurance, Stevens Point, Wis.

9.4 Senator Charles Mathias, quoted in American Bar Association, *supra* note 9.2 at p. 2.

9.5 "Status and Characteristics of Data Protection Legislation," *Transnational Data Report*, Vol. 3, No. 2, June 1980, pp. 15–18.

9.6 Organization for Economic Cooperation and Development, *Recommendation of the Council Concerning Guidelines Governing the Protection of Privacy and Transborder Flows of Personal Data* (adopted by the Council at its 523rd meeting, September 23, 1980), Paris, October 1, 1980.

9.7 Oswald H. Ganley, *The United States–Canadian Communications and Information Resources Relationship and its Possible Significance for Worldwide Diplomacy*, Program on Information Resources Policy, Harvard University, Cambridge, February 1980.

9.8 McCaffery, Seligman & von Simson, Inc., *Impact of Transborder Data Flow Legislation: Research Team Observations Based on Corporate Case Studies*, October 1979.

9.9 U.S. Congress, House Committee on Government Operations, *International Information Flow: Forging a New Framework*, House Report 96–1535, 96th Cong., 2d Sess., December 11, 1980.

9.10 International Chamber of Commerce Commission on Multinational Enterprises, *Regulations of International Information Flows*, Document No. 191/124.

9.11 Intergovernmental Bureau for Informatics, *Issues on Transborder Data Flow Policies*, Green Series—Documents on Policies for Informatics, September 1979.

9.12 SARK (a Swedish government committee), *The Vulnerability of the Computerized Society: Consideration and Proposals*, trans. John Hogg, LiberTryck, Stockholm, 1979. This is the summary in English of a report by a Swedish government committee, Sarbarhetskommitten (SARK). The title of the report in Swedish is *ADB och samhallets sarbarhet, overvaganden och forslag.* The report was published in December 1979 (SOU 1979:93); *TDF News,* Vol. 3, No. 5, May 1980.

10 Dividing Up the Spectrum: WARC '79

10.1 Rosemary Righter, "Battle of the Bias," *Foreign Policy,* Vol. 34, Spring 1979, pp. 121–138; Anne W. Branscomb, "Waves of the Future: Making WARC Work," *Foreign Policy,* Vol. 34, Spring 1979, pp. 139–148; Curtis T. White, "Uprooting the Squatters," *Foreign Policy,* Vol. 34, Spring 1979, pp. 148–153; Francis S. Ronalds, Jr., "Voices of America," *Foreign Policy,* Vol. 34, Spring 1979, pp. 155–164.

10.2 U.S. Department of State, *The U.S. Proposals for the 1979 World Administrative Radio Conference: An Executive Summary.*

10.3 Jake Kirchner, "Conference Panel Calls WARC a U.S. Success," *Computerworld,* February 18, 1980, p. 64; Wilson Dizard, *WARC-79 and Communications Satellites: An American Perspective,* paper presented at the On Line Conference on Communications Satellites, London, June 18, 1980.

10.4 S. J. Lukasik, *What Happened at WARC,* personal communication, January 1980; U.S. Department of State, *World Administrative Radio Conference,* Summary Report No. 9, December 1979; Federal Communications Commission, *Staff Report to the Commission on the Results of the 1979 World Administrative Radio Conference,* January 15, 1980.

10.5. Glen O. Robinson, *Report of the Chairman of the United States Delegation to the World Administrative Radio Conference of the International Telecommunication Union* (Geneva, September 24–December 6, 1979), U.S. Department of State, Office of International Communications Policy, TD Serial No. 116.

10.6 Arthur Freeman, personal communications.

11 Expanding International Satellite Capabilities and Two Controversial Activities

11.1 "Satellites—Eurobirds," *The Economist,* January 10, 1981, p. 58.

11.2 Eric Novotny, personal communications.

11.3   International Telecommunications Satellite Organization, *Annual Report,* 1979.

11.4   Irving Goldstein, *supra* note 2.12.

11.5   "Chipping the Cost," *The Economist,* September 20, 1980, p. 106.

11.6   Communications Satellite Corporation, *COMSAT Guide to the INTELSAT, MARISAT and COMSTAR Satellite Systems,* Washington, D.C.

11.7   John H. Chapman and Gabriel I. Warren, "Direct Broadcast Satellites: The ITU, UN and the Real World," *Annals of Air and Space Law,* Vol. IV, 1979, Centre for Research, Institute of Air and Space Law, McGill University, Montreal, p. 413.

11.8   Jonathan Gunter, *supra* note 7.12 at p. 21.

11.9   International Telecommunication Union, *1976 Edition of Radio Regulations,* Vol. 2: *Resolutions,* Geneva.

11.10   *Principles Governing the Use by States of Artificial Earth Satellites for Direct Television Broadcasting* (Canadian-Swedish Compromise), January 1979.

11.11   Stephen E. Doyle, *supra* note 2.13; U.S. Congress, House Committee on Science and Technology, International Space Activities, 1979, Hearings before the Subcommittee on Space Science and Applications, 96th Cong., 1st Sess., September 5 and 6, 1979.

11.12   U.S. President, *Presidential Directive/NSC-54,* November 16, 1979; U.S. Department of Commerce, *Planning for a Civil Operational Land Remote Sensing Satellite System: A Discussion of Issues and Options,* June 20, 1980.

12   Communications and Information Resources in Development

12.1   National Research Council, *U.S. Science and Technology for Development: A Contribution to the 1979 U.N. Conference* (Background Study on Suggested U.S. Initiatives for the U.N. Conference on Science and Technology for Development, Vienna, 1979), Government Printing Office, Washington, D.C., 1978

12.2   U.S. Congress (Senate) *Reports Submitted to Congress Pursuant to the Foreign Relations Authorization Act, Fiscal Year 1979 (Public Law 95–426),* 96th Cong., 1st Sess., July 1979, pp. 93–95.

12.3   Ibid.

12.4   Robert J. Saunders, *Financing of Telecommunication Expansion,* P.U. Report No. PUN 48, September 1979.

12.5   ABC, *Good Morning, America,* October 22, 1980, Interview with Robert McNamara; "McNamara: US Fails the Poor," *Boston Globe,* October 1, 1980.

12.6   Hans Otto Kaufman, "World Telephone Network Expands 6% to 7% Every Year," *Inteltrade,* Vol. 2, No. 23, December 15, 1979, pp. 6–7.

12.7   "Egypt Lets Pact to Modernize Communications System," *Inteltrade,* Vol. 2, No. 19, October 15, 1979, pp. 1–3; Youssef M. Ibrahim, "Extensive Network's Cost is $7 Billion," *New York Times,* March 20, 1980.

12.8   Robert J. Saunders and C. R. Dickenson, *Telecommunications: Priority Needs for Economic Development,* P.U. Report No. PUN 45A, June 1979.

12.9   Aspen Institute Program on Communications and Society, *Problems in International Communications: Conference Report,* Aspen Institute, Washington, D.C., 1978.

12.10   Robert J. Saunders and C. R. Dickenson, *supra* note 12.8.

12.11   U.S. Congress, Senate Committee on Foreign Relations, *International Communications and Information, Hearings before the Subcommittee on International Operations,* 95th Cong., 1st Sess., June 8, 9, and 10, 1977.

12.12   Aspen Institute, *supra* note 12.9.

12.13   ABC, *supra* note 12.5.

12.14   Majid Tehranian, "Iran: Communication, Alienation, Revolution," *InterMedia,* Vol. 7, No. 6, March 1979.

13   Electronic Security and Defense Systems, Including Command, Control, Communications, and Intelligence (C³I)

13.1   James Feron, "The Profits in Fighter Systems: Loral Thrives on Orders for Electronic Gear," *New York Times,* June 26, 1980.

13.2   C. Kenneth Allard, *Intelligence and Arms Control: Process and Priorities,* unpublished paper, Kennedy School of Government, Harvard University, Spring 1980.

13.3   Personal communications with several knowledgeable sources.

13.4   Thomas Leney, "Overview of Strategic Command, Control, Communications and Intelligence," in *Seminar on Command, Control, Communications and Intelligence: Student Papers—Spring*

1980, Program on Information Resources Policy, Harvard University, Cambridge, Incidental Paper I-81-1, January 1981.

13.5   Ibid.

13.6   U.S. Congress, Senate Committee on Armed Services, *Recent False Alerts from the Nation's Missile Attack Warning System. Report of Senator Gary Hart and Senator Barry Goldwater*, 96th Cong., 2d Sess., October 9, 1980.

13.7   "That Nuclear Alarm Wasn't False" (editorial), *New York Times,* June 30, 1980; "Doomsday by Short-Circuit?" *The Economist,* June 14, 1980, p. 18.

13.8   James M. Ennes, Jr., *Assault on the Liberty: The True Story of the Israeli Attack on an American Intelligence Ship*, Random House, New York, 1979.

13.9   Raymond Tate, "Worldwide C³I and Telecommunications," in *Seminar on Command, Control, Communications and Intelligence: Guest Presentations—Spring 1980*, Program on Information Resources Policy, Harvard University, Cambridge, Incidental Paper I-80-6, December 1980.

13.10   Ibid.

13.11   Ibid.

13.12   U.S. Department of Defense, Special Operations Review Group, *Rescue Mission Report,* August 1980.

13.13   Norman Polmar, "Thinking About Soviet C³," *NATO's Fifteen Nations,* October-November 1979, p. 36.

14   Arms Control and the Role of Communications and Information in Peacekeeping

14.1   U.S. Arms Control and Disarmament Agency, *Arms Control and Disarmament Agreements*, 1977 ed., p. 134.

14.2   Ray S. Cline, *The CIA under Reagan, Bush and Casey: The Evolution of an Agency from Roosevelt to Reagan*, Acropolis Books Ltd., Washington, D.C., 1981.

14.3   Anthony G. Oettinger, "Information Resources: Knowledge and Power in the 21st Century," *Science*, Vol. 209, July 4, 1980, pp. 191–198.

14.4   Les Aspin, "The Verification of the SALT II Agreement," *Scientific American*, Vol. 240, February 1979, p. 8.

14.5   U.S. Congress, Senate Committee on Foreign Relations, *The Salt II Treaty. Hearings before the Committee on Foreign Relations on EX. Y, 96–1,* Part 2, 96th Cong., 1st Sess., July 16, 17, 18, and 19, 1979, p. 242.

14.6 William E. Colby, Testimony before U.S. Congress, Senate Committee on Foreign Relations, *supra* note 12.11 at pp. 15–20.

14.7 *U.S. Department of State Bulletin,* September 29, 1975; Barry Cherniavsky, *Early Warning Systems and the American Peacekeeping Mission: The Case of the Sinai II Agreement Between Egypt and Israel,* Program on Information Resources Policy, Harvard University, Cambridge, Publication I–81–6, July 1981.

14.8 *U.S. Department of State Bulletin,* June 1978, p. 34.

15 The Widening Role of Electronic Codes, Message Interception, and Message Protection

15.1 Thomas Leney, *supra* note 13.4.

15.2 David Kahn, "Cryptology Goes Public," *Foreign Affairs,* Fall 1979, pp. 141–159.

15.3 *Treaty on the Limitation of Strategic Offensive Arms (SALT II Treaty),* June 18, 1979.

15.4 Greg Lipscomb, *Private and Public Defenses Against Soviet Interception of U.S. Telecommunications: Problems and Policy Points,* Program on Information Resources Policy, Harvard University, Cambridge, Publication P-79-3, July 1979.

15.5 John M. Geddes, "East German Espionage Said to Focus on Western Micro-electronic Industry," *Wall Street Journal,* June 6, 1980.

15.6 David Kahn, *supra* note 15.2.

15.7 U.S. Department of Commerce, National Bureau of Standards, *Data Encryption Standard,* FIPS Publication 46, January 15, 1977, p. 156.

16 U.S.–Canadian Communications and Information Relationships as a Case Study

16.1 During 1978–79, an extensive study of U.S.–Canadian communications and information relationships was conducted by the first author under the auspices of the Harvard Program on Information Resources Policy. U.S.–Canadian general relationships were found to be indeed close, and their communications and information relationships have certain seemingly unique features by virtue of geographic proximity and relatively similar needs and tastes. But the controversial and cooperative issues found to exist between the two countries were considered to be in no way exceptional to those now present or which can be expected to crop up soon between the United States and other nations. Some details of that relationship are therefore included here as a guide to what can be expected to develop elsewhere around the world in the course of the coming few years; Oswald H. Ganley, *supra* note 7.6; Oswald H. Ganley, *supra* note 9.7.

16.2   *Home Video Report,* Vol. 11, No. 4, January 26, 1981, p. 3.

16.3   Canada, House of Commons, Bill C-6 (An Act to revise the Bank Act . . .), 32d Parliament, 1st Sess., 1980. (Adopted November 19, 1980.)

16.4   U.S. President, Message to the Congress, September 9, 1980.

16.5   SBS launched the first of its three satellites on November 15, 1980. In December 1980, SBS filed a petition with the FCC to extend SBS service to Canada.

17   U.S.–Advanced Country Communications and Information Relationships

17.1   Colin Norman, *Microelectronics at Work: Productivity and Jobs in the World Economy,* Worldwatch Paper 39, Worldwatch Institute, Washington, D.C., October 1980; CIPS Review, January/ February 1980; numerous articles in the general and specialized press in OECD countries have appeared on this subject in recent years.

17.2   "The Chip Is Not a Ferret" (editorial), *InterMedia,* September 1980.

17.3   *Inteltrade,* December 15, 1979, p. 15.

18   U.S.–Communist Country Communications and Information Relationships

18.1   U.S. Arms Control and Disarmament Agency, *supra* note 14.1.

18.2   Personal communications, various sources.

18.3   U.S. Department of Defense, Office of Assistant Secretary of Defense (Public Affairs), *News Release,* January 24, 1980; U.S. Department of Commerce, "Commerce Secretary Denies $1 Billion

Plus in Export Licenses for Soviet Union," *News Release*, G-80-9, January 11, 1980; Idem, "President Sets Tougher Criteria on High Technology Exports to the U.S.S.R., *News Release*, G-80-55, March 19, 1980; U.S. Departments of State and Commerce, *Questions/ Answers on U.S. Export Policy Towards the USSR*, March 28, 1980.

18.4   Eric Novotny, personal communications.

19   U.S.–Developing Country Communications and Information Relationships

19.1   ABC, *supra* note 12.5.

19.2   William Sweet, "Third World Debts," *Congressional Quarterly*, Vol. II, No. 4, July 25, 1980.

19.3   "Vital Statistics of the Planet," *New York Times*, December 30, 1979.

19.4   ABC, *supra* note 12.5; John W. Sewell et al., *The United States and World Development: Agenda 1980*, Praeger Publishers, New York, N.Y., 1980; William J. Broad, "UN at Odds over Science Center," *Science*, Vol. 207, January 25, 1980, pp. 387–391.

19.5   Irving Goldstein, "Satellites and Third World Communication Systems: Opportunities and Pitfalls," presentation before the US-Japan Symposium, The Fletcher School of Diplomacy, Tufts University, Medford, Mass., October 1979.

20   The International Policy Environment of Communications and Information Resources

20.1   Richard F. Janssen, "Even on the Back Roads of the Ozarks, Trade Issues Take on New Prominence," *Wall Street Journal*, November 14, 1980.

20.2   U.S. Department of Defense, Defense Science Task Board on Export of U.S. Technology, *An Analysis of Export Control of U.S. Technology—a DoD Perspective (Bucy Report)*, February 4, 1976.

20.3   Computer and Business Equipment Manufacturers Association, personal communications.

Bibliography

1 The Birth of a New Economic Sector

Actes Du Colloque International Informatique et Société. 5 vols. La Documentation Francaise, Paris, 1980. Vol. 1: *Informatisation et Changement Economique.* Vol. 2: *Informatique Travail et Emploi.* Vol. 3: *Informatique Télématique et Vie Quotidienne.* Vol. 4: *Informatique Cooperation Internationale et Independence.* Vol. 5: *Informatique et Democratie.*

Bell, Daniel. "Communications Technology—For Better or for Worse," *Harvard Business Review,* May–June 1979, p. 20 ff.

Bergsten, C. Fred, Thomas Horst, and Theodore H. Moran. *American Multinationals and American Interests,* The Brookings Institution, Washington, D.C., 1978.

Brzezinski, Zbigniew. *Statement for French Conference on Informatique et Société,* September 18, 1979.

Economist Intelligence Unit Ltd. *Chips in the 1980s: The Application of Micro-Electronic Technology in Products for Consumer and Business Markets,* EIU Special Report No. 67, EIU, London, England, 1979.

Edelstein, Alex S., John E. Bowes, and Sheldon M. Harsel. *Information Societies: Comparing the Japanese and American Experiences,* International Communication Center, University of Washington, Seattle, 1978.

Ganley, Oswald H. *Current Problems of Science and Technology Affecting U.S.–European Relations*, Spring 1968 (unpublished paper).

Ganley, Oswald H. "U.S. Policy on International Research and Development," in Engineering Foundation, *Proceedings of a Conference on Engineering and Science Research for Industrial Development*, Easton, Md., October 3–7, 1977, pp. 195–201.

Gotlieb, C. C., and Z. P. Zeman. *Towards a National Computer and Communications Policy: Seven National Approaches*, Institute for Research on Public Policy, Toronto, May 1980.

Granger, John V. *Technology and International Relations*, W. H. Freeman and Co., San Francisco, 1979.

Hershey, Robert D., Jr. "Foreigners' Investment: A Warning," *New York Times*, August 8, 1980.

Lecht, Charles P. *The Waves of Change: A Techno-Economic Analysis of the Data Processing Industry*, Advanced Computer Techniques Corporation, New York, 1977.

McLaughlin, John F., with Anne E. Birinyi. *Mapping the Information Business*, Program on Information Resources Policy, Harvard University, Cambridge, Publication P-80-5, July 1980.

Ministry of International Trade and Industry. *The Vision of MITI Policies in 1980s: Summary* (Provisional Translation), NR-226 (80–7), March 17, 1980.

National Science Board. *Science Indicators—1978: Report of the National Science Board*, Government Printing Office, Washington, D.C., 1979.

Nora, Simon, and Alain Minc. *The Computerization of Society: A Report to the President of France*, MIT Press, Cambridge, 1980.

Oettinger, Anthony G., Paul J. Berman, and William H. Read. *High and Low Politics: Information Resources for the '80s*, Ballinger Publishing Co., Cambridge, 1977.

Organization for Economic Co-operation and Development. *Group of Experts on Economic Analysis of Information Activities and the Role of Electronics and Telecommunications Technologies*, Vol. 2: *Background Reports*, OECD, Paris, June 30, 1980.

Organization for Economic Co-operation and Development. *Handbook of Information Computer and Communications Activities of Major International Organizations*, OECD, Paris, 1980.

Organization for Economic Co-operation and Development. *Information Activities, Electronics and Telecommunications Technologies—Impacts on Employment, Growth and Trade*, Vol. 1: *Part A:*

Executive Summary. Part B: Analytical Report, OECD, Paris, September 1, 1980.

Organization for Economic Co-operation and Development. *Technical Change and Economic Policy: Science and Technology in the New Economic and Social Context,* OECD, Paris, 1980.

Porat, Marc U. "The U.S. as an Information Society: International Implications," in *Selected Papers: International Policy Implications of Computers and Advanced Telecommunications in Information Systems,* U.S. Department of State, January 1979, pp. 14–32.

Rudenberg, H. Gunther. *World Semiconductor Industry in Transition: 1978–1983,* Arthur D. Little, Cambridge, February 1980.

Servan-Schreiber, J. J. *The American Challenge,* Atheneum, New York, 1968.

Toffler, Alvin. *Future Shock,* Random House, New York, 1970.

U.S. Congress. House Committee on Government Operations. *The Adequacy of the Federal Response to Foreign Investment in the United States,* H. Rept. 96–1216, 96th Cong., 2d Sess., 1980.

U.S. Congress. House Committee on Government Operations. *The Operations of Federal Agencies in Monitoring, Reporting On, and Analyzing Foreign Investments in the United States* (Part 5—Appendices). *Hearings before a Subcommittee of the Committee on Government Operations,* 95th Cong., 1st Sess., September 19, 20, 21, 1978; July 16, 17, 18, 26, 30, 31; and August 1, 1979.

U.S. Congress. House Committee on House Administration. *Information Policy: Public Laws from the 95th Congress,* 96th Cong., 1st Sess., January 31, 1979.

U.S. Congress. House Committee on Science and Technology. *Seminar on Research, Productivity and the National Economy,* 96th Cong., 2d Sess., June 18, 1980.

U.S. Congress. House Committee on Ways and Means, Subcommittee on Trade. *United States-Japan Trade Report,* WMCP: 96–68, 96th Cong., 2d Sess., September 5, 1980.

U.S. Department of Commerce. Office of Telecommunications. *The Information Economy: Definition and Measurement,* by Marc Uri Porat, OT Special Publication 77–12 (1), Government Printing Office, Washington, D.C., 1977.

Vogel, Ezra F. *Japan as Number One: Lessons for America,* Harvard University Press, Cambridge, 1979.

Winpisinger, William H. "The Case Against Exporting US Technology," *Research Management,* March 1978, p. 19.

Zurkowski, Paul G. *Communications, Information Resources and the Economy,* remarks made at the National Information Conference and Exposition, April 29, 1979.

2 Specific International Problem Areas

Banker, Stephen, "For Cable TV, It's a One-Way Border," *TV Guide,* January 12, 1980, pp. 31–36.

Brown, George E., Jr. *Freedom and Order in Future International Communications,* paper presented at the 43rd annual meeting of the U.S. National Commission for UNESCO, Athens, Ga., December 12–15, 1979.

Clippinger, John H. *Who Gains by Communications Development? Studies of Information Technologies in Developing Countries,* Program on Information Resources Policy, Harvard University, Cambridge, Working Paper 76–1, January 1976.

Communications Satellite Corporation. *Report to the President and the Congress,* 1979.

Council of Europe. European Committee on Legal Co-operation. Report of 33rd Meeting (Strasbourg, June 23–27, 1980), Addendum I: *Protection of Individuals with Regard to Automatic Processing of Personal Data,* CDCJ (80) 28, Strasbourg, July 24, 1980.

Dimensions of Privacy, The, a national opinion research survey of attitudes toward privacy, Sentry Insurance, New York, May 1980.

Duke, Robin Chandler. *General Policy Statement,* presented at the 21st General Conference of UNESCO, Belgrade, September 26, 1980.

Eger, John, "Dams in the Data Stream," *New York Times,* August 21, 1979.

Ennes, James M., Jr. *Assault on the Liberty: The True Story of the Israeli Attack on an American Intelligence Ship,* Random House, New York, 1979.

"Evolution of the International Code of Conduct to Govern Remote Sensing by Satellite, The," *Annals of Air and Space Law,* Vol. III, 1978, pp. 561–574.

Fishman, William L. "Introduction to Transborder Data Flows," *Stanford Journal of International Law,* Vol. XVI, Summer 1980, pp. 1–26.

Fishman, William L. *National Telecommunications and Information Administration (NTIA),* remarks presented to the American Society of International Law, Washington, D.C., April 18, 1980.

Ganley, Oswald H. *Transborder Data Flow—Some Problems of Privacy vs. Freedom of Information and Economic Issues,* an address to CBEMA, Phoenix, Ariz., March 20, 1978.

Goldstein, Irving. *Satellites and Third World Communication Systems: Opportunities and Pitfalls,* presentation before the US-Japan Symposium, The Fletcher School of Diplomacy, Tufts University, Medford, Mass., October 1979.

"Great Information War, The," *Foreign Policy,* Vol. 34, 1979, pp. 120–164.

Gunter, Jonathan F., and Timothy J. Logue. *LDC Expressions of Concerns and Requirements Re the 1979 WARC,* Academy of Educational Development, January 16, 1979.

Harris, Louis, *The Dimension of Privacy,* remarks at Sentry Press Conference, New York, May 3, 1979.

Hoffman, Lance J. (ed.). *Computers and Privacy in the Next Decade,* Academic Press, New York, 1980.

Inman, B. R. *The NSA Perspective on Telecommunications Protection in the Nongovernmental Sector,* public address, n.d.

International Commission for the Study of Communication Problems. *Final Report (MacBride Report),* Part Five: *Communication Tomorrow* (Conclusions and Recommendations), Paris, 1980.

International Telecommunications Satellite Organization. *Annual Report,* 1979.

International Telecommunication Union. *Final Acts of the 1979 World Administrative Radio Conference, Geneva, 1979* (Unofficial Version), Vol. II: *Appendices, Resolutions and Recommendations,* National Technical Information Service, Springfield, Va., 1979.

Kroloff, George, and Scott Cohen. *The New World Information Order,* a report submitted to the Committee on Foreign Relations, U.S. Senate, November 1977.

Lipscomb, Greg. *Private and Public Defenses Against Soviet Interception of U.S. Telecommunications: Problems and Policy Points,* Program on Information Resources Policy, Harvard University, Cambridge, Publication P-79–3, July 1979.

Madec, Alain J. *Economic and Legal Aspects of Transborder Data Flows (1),* DSTI/ICCP/80.26, Commission on Transborder Data Flows (A French Government Interdepartmental Working Party).

Masmoudi, M. Mustapha. *The New World Information Order,* an address for the International Commission for the Study of Communication Problems, Paris, July 10–12, 1978.

Matte, Nicolas M., and Hamilton DeSaussure (eds.). *Legal Implications of Remote Sensing from Outer Space*, Sijthoff, Leyden, 1976.

National Research Council. *Resource Sensing from Space: Prospects for Developing Countries*. National Academy of Sciences, Washington, D.C., 1977.

National Research Council. *Technology, Trade, and the U.S. Economy: Report of a Workshop Held at Woods Hole, Massachusetts, August 22–31, 1976*, National Academy of Sciences, Washington, D.C., 1978.

National Research Council. *U.S. Science and Technology for Development: A Contribution to the 1979 U.N. Conference* (Background Study on Suggested U.S. Initiatives for the U.N. Conference on Science and Technology for Development, Vienna, 1979), Government Printing Office, Washington, D.C., 1978.

Organization for Economic Co-operation and Development. *Expert Group on Transborder Data Barriers and the Protection of Privacy—Explanatory Memorandum*, DSTI/ICCP/79.41, July 23, 1979.

Organization for Economic Co-operation and Development. *Recommendation of the Council Concerning Guidelines Governing Protection of Privacy and Transborder Flows of Personal Data* (adopted by the Council at its 523rd meeting, September 23, 1980), October 1, 1980.

Ostry, Bernard. *The Cultural Connection: An Essay on Culture and Government Policy in Canada*, with an introduction by Robert Fulford, McClelland and Stewart, Toronto, Canada, 1978.

Pinch, Edward T. "A Brief Study of News Patterns in Sixteen Third World Countries," *Murrow Reports: Occasional Papers of the Edward R. Murrow Center of Public Diplomacy*, Tufts University, Medford, Mass., March 1978.

Pool, Ithiel de Sola. *The US Faces WARC*, paper presented at the Sixth Annual Telecommunications Policy Research Conference, Airlie House, May 12, 1978.

Queeney, Kathryn. *Direct Broadcast Satellites and the U.N.*, Sijthoff & Noordhoff, Leyden, 1978.

Read, William H. *America's Mass Media Merchants*, Johns Hopkins University Press, Baltimore, 1976.

Read, William H. *The First Amendment Meets the Second Revolution*, Program on Information Resources Policy, Harvard University, Cambridge, Publication P-81-1, 1981.

Reinhardt, John E. *Towards an Acceptable Concept of the New*

World Information Order, an address for the US-Japan Symposium, The Fletcher School of Diplomacy, Tufts University, Medford, Mass., October 11, 1979.

Righter, Rosemary. *Whose News? Politics, the Press and the Third World,* Times Books, New York, 1978.

Robinson, Glen O. (ed.). *Communications for Tomorrow: Policy Perspectives for the 1980s,* Praeger Publishers, New York, 1978.

Robinson, Glen O. *1979 World Administrative Radio Conference.* Statement before U.S. Congress. House Committee on Science and Technology, Sub-committee on Space Science and Applications, September 6, 1979.

Schiller, Herbert I. *Mass Communications and American Empire,* Augustus Kelley, New York, 1969.

Seminar on Command, Control, Communications and Intelligence: Guest Presentations—Spring 1980, Program on Information Resources Policy, Harvard University, Cambridge, Incidental Paper I-80-6, December 1980.

Seminar on Command, Control, Communications and Intelligence: Student Papers—Spring 1980, Program on Information Resources Policy, Harvard University, Cambridge, Incidental Paper I-81-1, January 1981.

Smith, Delbert D. *Space Stations: International Law and Policy,* Westview Press, Boulder, Colo., 1977.

Solomon, Richard Jay. *World Communications Facts: A Handbook Prepared for the International Conference on World Communications: Decisions for the 80s,* Annenberg School of Communications, University of Pennsylvania, Philadelphia, 1980.

Stanford Journal of International Law, Vol. XVI: Transborder Data Flow, Summer 1980.

"Struggle over the World's Radio Waves Will Continue, The," *The Economist,* December 4, 1979.

Terrell, Norman. *On Planning for a Civil Operational Land Remote Sensing Satellite System.* Statement before U.S. Congress. Senate, Committee on Commerce, Science and Transportation, Sub-committee on Science, Technology and Space, July 24, 1980.

Turn, Rein (ed.). *Transborder Data Flows: Concerns in Privacy Protection and Free Flow of Information,* Vol. 1: *Report of the AFIPS Panel on Transborder Data Flow,* American Federation of Information Processing Societies, Arlington, Va., 1979.

Tyler, Michael. *The Planning and Justification of Investment in*

Telecommunications, paper presented at the International Telecommunication Union's World Telecommunication Forum, September 1979.

UNESCO. *Text of Consensus Resolution of the Intergovernmental Meeting on Communications Development: Draft Version,* April 21, 1980.

"UNESCO 21st General Conference in Belgrade: An InterMedia Special Report," *InterMedia,* November 1980.

United Nations. General Assembly, 3rd session, December 10, 1948. *Universal Declaration of Human Rights,* Article 19.

U.S. Congress. House Committee on Foreign Affairs. *North-South Dialog: Progress and Prospects. Hearings before the Subcommittees on International Economic Policy and Trade and on International Organizations,* 96th Cong., 2d Sess., May 1, 13, 15, and June 19, 1980.

U.S. Congress. House Committee on Government Operations. *International Information Flow: Forging a New Framework,* H. Rept. 96–1535, 96th Cong., 2d Sess., 1980.

U.S. Congress. Senate Committee on Armed Services. *Recent False Alerts from the Nation's Missile Attack Warning System. Report of Senator Gary Hart and Senator Barry Goldwater,* 96th Cong., 2d Sess., October 9, 1980.

U.S. Congress. Senate Committee on Commerce, Science and Transportation. *Space Law: Selected Basic Documents,* 2d ed. Committee Print. 95th Cong., 2d Sess., December 1978.

U.S. Congress. Senate Committee on Foreign Relations. *International Communications and Information. Hearings before the Subcommittee on International Operations,* 95th Cong., 1st Sess., June 8, 9, and 10, 1977.

U.S. Congress. Senate Committee on Foreign Relations. *The SALT II Treaty. Hearings on Ex. Y, 96–1,* Pts. 1–4, 96th Cong., 1st Sess., 1979.

U.S. Congress (Senate). *Reports Submitted to Congress Pursuant to the Foreign Relations Authorization Act, Fiscal Year 1979 (Public Law 95–426),* 96th Cong., 1st sess., July 1979.

U.S. Department of Commerce. Office of Telecommunications. *Selected Foreign National Data Protection Laws and Bills,* ed. by Charles K. Wilk, OT Special Publication 78–19, Government Printing Office, Washington, D.C., 1978.

U.S. Department of Commerce. *Planning for a Civil Operational*

Land Remote Sensing Satellite System: A Discussion of Issues and Options, June 20, 1980.

U.S. Department of Defense. Office of Assistant Secretary of Defense (Public Affairs). "Remarks Prepared for Delivery by the Honorable Harold Brown, Secretary of Defense, at the Convocation Ceremonies for the 97th Naval War College Class, Naval War College, Newport, Rhode Island, August 20, 1980," *News Release* (No. 344–80).

U.S. Department of State. Bureau of Oceans and International Environmental and Scientific Affairs. *Selected Papers: International Policy Implications of Computers and Advanced Telecommunications in Information Systems,* January 1979.

U.S. Department of State. Bureau of Public Affairs. *SALT II Agreement.* Vienna, June 18, 1979. (Selected Documents No. 12B.)

U.S. Department of State. National Commission for UNESCO. *Toward an American Agenda for a New World Order of Communications,* National Commission for UNESCO, Washington, D.C., January 1980.

U.S. Department of State. *The US Proposal for the 1979 World Administrative Radio Conference: An Executive Summary,* June 1979.

U.S. Department of State. *World Administrative Radio Conference,* Summary Report No. 7.

U.S. Department of State. *World Administrative Radio Conference,* Summary Report No. 9.

U.S. Science and Technology for Development: A Contribution to the 1979 U.N. Conference, Government Printing Office, Washington, D.C., 1978.

"US Trade Negotiator to Lead United States Communication/Data Processing Bargaining," *Transnational Data Report,* Vol. III, No. 5, September 1980, pp. 7–8.

3   One Bilateral Relationship

Canada, Consultative Committee on the Implications of Telecommunications for Canadian Sovereignty. *Telecommunications and Canada* (Clyne Report), Ottawa, 1979.

Ganley, Oswald H. *The Role of Communications and Information Resources in Canada,* Program on Information Resources Policy, Harvard University, Cambridge, Publication P-79-1, June 1979.

Ganley, Oswald H. *The United States-Canadian Communications and Information Resources Relationship and Its Possible Significance for Worldwide Diplomacy,* Program on Information Resources Policy, Harvard University, Cambridge, February 1980.

U.S. President. *Message to the Congress,* September 9, 1980.

4   Communications and Information Resources in a Geopolitical Context

Agreement on the Establishment of the "Intersputnik" International System and Organization of Space Communications, Moscow, November 15, 1971.

Fisher, Glen. *American Communication in a Global Society,* Ablex Publishing Co., Norwood, N.J., 1979.

Group of Thirty. Exchange Markets Participants' Study Group. *The Foreign Exchange Markets Under Floating Rates: A Study in International Finance,* Group of Thirty, New York, 1980.

Group of Thirty. Reserve Assets Study Group. *Reserve Assets and a Substitution Account: Towards a Less Unstable International Monetary System,* Group of Thirty, New York, 1980.

Homet, Roland S., Jr. *Social and Political Dimensions of Communications Development,* an address presented at the US-Japan Symposium, The Fletcher School of Diplomacy, Tufts University, Medford, Mass., October 12, 1979.

International Commission for the Study of Communication Problems. *Some Remarks on the Relation between the New International Information Order and the New International Economic Order,* by Jan Pronk (No. 35), 1978.

International Commission for the Study of Communication Problems. *The New International Economic Order and the New International Information Order,* by Cees Hamelink (No. 34), 1978.

Meadows, Donella (ed.). *Limits to Growth: A Report for the Club of Rome's Project on the Predicament of Mankind,* 2d ed., Universe, New York, 1974.

North-South: A Program for Survival: Report of the Independent Commission on International Development Issues, by Willy Brandt, Chairman, MIT Press, Cambridge, 1980.

Pinder, John, Takashi Hosomi, and William Diebold. *Industrial Policy and the International Economy: Report of the Trilateral Task*

Force on Industrial Policy to the Trilateral Commission. The Triangle Papers: 19, The Trilateral Commission, New York, 1979.

Sewell, John W., et al. *The United States and World Development: Agenda 1980,* Praeger Publishers, New York, 1980.

Smith, Anthony. *The Geopolitics of Information: How Western Culture Dominates the World,* Oxford University Press, New York, 1980.

Statement, C. Clyde Ferguson, Jr., Head, United States Delegation to the 31st session of ECOSOC, New Delhi, February 28, 1975.

U.S. Central Intelligence Agency. *National Basic Intelligence Factbook,* Government Printing Office, Washington, D.C., January 1980.

U.S. Congress. Office of Technology Assessment. *Technology and East-West Trade,* Government Printing Office, Washington, D.C., November 1979.

U.S. Department of State. Bureau of Intelligence and Research. *Status of the World's Nations,* Geographic Bulletin (Revised), Pubn. 8735, September 1980.

"Vital Statistics of the Planet," *New York Times,* December 30, 1979.

5 Eighteen Points for Formulating Policy

Drucker, Peter F. *The Age of Discontinuity: Guidelines to Our Changing Society,* Harper & Row, New York, 1969.

Duignan, Peter and Rabushka (eds.). *The United States in the 1980s,* Hoover Institution, Stanford, Publication 228, 1980.

Juneau, Pierre. *National Information in the Global Environment,* an address to the Workshop on Strategic Implications of the Changing Telecommunications Environment of Newspapers, Program on Information Resources Policy, Harvard University, Cambridge, November 11, 1980.

LeGates, John C., et al. *Foreign Policy Choices for the 1970s and 1980s: Information Resources Strategic Strengths—Strategic Weaknesses,* Program on Information Resources Policy, Harvard University, Cambridge, Publication P-76-6, October 1976.

Pelton, Joseph N., and Marcellus S. Snow (eds.). *Economic and Policy Problems in Satellite Communications,* Praeger, New York, 1978.

Read, William H. *Communications Policy: An Agenda,* Program on Information Resources Policy, Harvard University, Cambridge, Working Paper W-77–4, May 1977

Read, William H. *Foreign Policy: The High and Low Politics of Telecommunications,* Program on Information Resources Policy, Harvard University, Cambridge, Publication P-76–3, February 1976.

Read, William H. *Rethinking International Communications,* Program on Information Resources Policy, Harvard University, Cambridge, Publication P-78–1, April 1978.

Toffler, Alvin. *The Third Wave,* William Morrow, New York, 1980.

U.S. Congress. Senate Committee on Foreign Relations. *Foreign Relations Authorization Act, Fiscal Year 1978* (Section 402), May 15, 1978.

U.S. Congress. Senate Committee on Foreign Relations. *Foreign Relations Authorization Act, Fiscal Year 1979* (Sections 402 and 404), S. Rept. 95–842, 95th Cong., 1979.

U.S. Department of Commerce. National Telecommunications and Information Administration. *The Foundations of United States Information Policy* (A United States Government Submission to the High-Level Conference on Information, Computer, and Communications Policy, Organization for Economic Cooperation and Development, Paris, October 6–8, 1980), by Arthur A. Bushkin and Jane H. Yurow, NTIA-SP-80–8, NTIA, Washington, D.C., June 1980.

U.S. President. "International Communication Agency," *Executive Order 12048* (FR Doc. 78–8496), March 27, 1978, in *Federal Register,* Vol. 43, No. 61, March 29, 1978, pp. 13361–13362.

U.S. President. "Relating to the Transfer of Telecommunications Functions," *Executive Order 12046* (FR Doc. 78–8494), March 27, 1978, in *Federal Register,* Vol. 43, No. 61, March 29, 1978, pp. 13349–13357.

U.S. President. *Reorganization Plan No. 2 of 1977,* October 11, 1977.

Vernon, R., and L. T. Wells. *Manager in the International Economy,* 3d ed., Prentice-Hall, Englewood Cliffs, N.J., 1976.

Vernon, Raymond. *Storm Over the Multinationals,* Harvard University Press, Cambridge, 1977.

Acronyms

ABM	Antiballistic Missile
CCITT	Consultative Committee for International Telephone and Telegraph of the International Telecommunication Union (ITU)
C³I	Command, Control, Communications, and Intelligence
CIA	Central Intelligence Agency
COCOM	Coordinating Committee
COE	Council of Europe
COMINT	Communications Intelligence
COMSEC	Communications Security
CRTC	Canadian Radio-television and Telecommunications Commission
CSCE	Conference on Security and Co-operation in Europe
DBS-TV	Direct Broadcast Satellite Television; also Direct Broadcasting by Satellite Television
DES	Data Encryption Standard
EC	European Community (sometimes European Economic Community)

ELINT	Electronic Intelligence
ESA	European Space Agency
FCC	Federal Communications Commission
GATT	General Agreement on Tariffs and Trade
GDP	Gross Domestic Product
GNP	Gross National Product
HF	High Frequency
IBI	Intergovernmental Bureau for Informatics
IIF	International Information Flow
INMARSAT	International Maritime Satellite organization
INTELSAT	International Telecommunications Satellite program
ITU	International Telecommunication Union (UN)
MARISAT	Marine Satellite (a global maritime communications system)
MTN	Multilateral Trade Negotiations
NASA	National Aeronautics and Space Administration
NCA	National Command Authority
NIEO	New International Economic Order
NIIO	New International Information Order
NSA	National Security Agency
NSC	National Security Council (USA)
NTIA	National Telecommunications and Information Administration
NWIO	New World Information Order
OECD	Organization for Economic Cooperation and Development
OPEC	Organization of Petroleum Exporting Countries
PSTN	Public Switched Telephone Network
PTT	Post, Telephone, and Telegraph Administrations; Post and Telecommunications Authorities; Posts, Telecommunications, and Telephones
SALT	Strategic Arms Limitation Talks
SBS	Satellite Business Systems is the consortium of COMSAT, IBM, and Aetna
SIGINT	Signal Intelligence

SPADE	Single Channel Per Carrier Pulse-Code Modulation-Accesses-Demand-Assigned Equipment (SCPC/SPADE)
TBDF	Transborder Data Flow
TDF	Transborder Data Flow
U-2	American intelligence-gathering plane
UK	United Kingdom
UNCSTD	United Nations Conference on Science and Technology for Development
UNESCO	United Nations Educational, Scientific and Cultural Organization
V-2	First guided missile, developed by Wernher von Braun in Baden-Wurttemberg, West Germany, during World War II
WARC	World Administrative Radio Conference

Index